D0975161

PRAISE FOR *Giving and Getting in the Kingdom*

Mark Dillon has done the church and ministry organizations a massive favor by articulating the essence and essentials of the art of gathering and giving in a clear and practical way. From a strong theological base, Mark charts the course for raising money God's way. As I read this book I became aware that this was not another theoretical treatment of a delicate subject but an unveiling of time-tested realities that have been Mark's modus operandi in his long and highly successful years at Wheaton College. This book is packed with practical advice and wise insights that will transform raising money from a dreaded task to a meaningful enterprise. Read this and you will agree that *Giving and Getting in the Kingdom* will become the gold standard for all of us who are called to the high calling of gathering for the advancement of the work of Christ.

—**JOSEPH STOWELL**
President, Cornerstone University

In *Giving and Getting in the Kingdom: A Field Guide*, Mark Dillon renders an invaluable service to the many constituents that comprise the phenomenon that is Christian philanthropy, including donors, ministers, educational leaders, board members, volunteers, fundraisers, and all those who are served by the compacts they form and purposes they pursue. No matter what your role, whether you are just beginning to fundraise or are fairly far down the road, the sooner you read this book, the surer and more joyous the remainder of your journey will become. Dillon is a wonderfully deft guide because he knows the landscape so well and has traversed it for decades with abiding faith, unflinching integrity, and deep humility. This book gives us the gift of knowing what this field is, or can be, at its very, very best.

—**JAMES M. LANGLEY**
President, Langley Innovations

If you want to lead your ministry to achieve its greatest potential for financial support, the guidebook is in your hands. Don't just read *Giving and Getting*, wear it out!"

—**JOHN C. MAXWELL**
Leadership expert and bestselling author

Mark Dillon gives a comprehensive look at professional development through the lens of biblical generosity. He shows how it is possible for a ministry to be utterly dependent on God's provision while at the same time strategically inviting God's people into His activity in the world.

—DENNY RYDBERG
President, Young Life

Mark Dillon's book focusing on developing financial support for kingdom purposes is a winner. I have witnessed firsthand Mark's skills in planning, launching, and completing several fund development initiatives—from a biblical perspective. His ideas are not merely theoretically sound but extremely practical for any sized institution.

—DR. MELVIN BANKS
Founder & Chairman, Urban Ministries, Inc.

I have had the great privilege and honor of knowing and being mentored by Mark Dillon for over sixteen years. I can testify that Mark is the real deal. As a leader of a small not-for-profit ministry, I have gleaned from him how to correctly infuse ministries with the necessary financial resources to advance God's kingdom on earth. Mark is all about doing things right before God's eyes, making Jesus Christ always look good for God's glory, regardless of the consequences. I call that biblical courage. We are living in times when biblical courage is greatly needed, as many ministries, churches, and Christian organizations are working to do the most with the least. *Giving and Getting in the Kingdom* provides the biblical perspective and approach in how to connect kingdom investors with their vision for the glory of King Jesus.

—MANNY MILL
Executive Director, Koinonia House® National Ministries

Mark Dillon has written a masterpiece on giving and generosity in the kingdom of God. Mark deals with the transformation of a giver's heart as the first step to radical giving. This book gives important guidelines for development teams as they work with donors.
I hope you read it, read it, and read it again.

—DON MEYER
Past Owner & President of the Baillie Lumber Company

Mark's deep wisdom and experience in fundraising and development provides an effective road map for both nonprofit organizations and donors alike. He explores the unique challenges of engaging successful, nonprofit organizations with generous, thoughtful givers with fresh and insightful perspectives from his many years of experience at one of the finest, educational institutions in the country.

—BONNIE WURZBACHER
Senior Vice President, Global Customer & Channel Leadership
The Coca-Cola Company

Wealth is a gift of God. In the absence of stewardship, it can become consuming and a peril of life. God's work in this world is dependent on responsible stewardship with a cheerful heart. How then can these principles of our faith work together to support the advancement of the kingdom of God? This is the subject that Mark Dillon addresses in a very thoughtful and skillful way in this book. His writing reflects years of experience and leadership in putting into practice what he says. My confidence in saying this reflects the opportunity I have had as a trustee of Wheaton College to work alongside him and observe his leadership in action.

—BILL POLLARD
Chairman, Fairwyn Investment Company, LLC

Mark Dillon is a faithful follower of Christ with a distinguished career, successfully raising resources for ministries, and he has concluded that the process of raising resources is to "plant" and "water" and "it is God who gives the increase." As he points out in this book, he has come to learn that to give as a faithful and generous steward of God's resources is to see God in, under, and through every aspect of the process and that the funding is attributed to the grace of God in Christ. My prayer is that as a result of this book, many resources will be raised to further God's eternal kingdom.

—WESLEY K. WILLMER, PH.D.
Author of God and Your Stuff, Revolution in Generosity,
The Prospering Parachurch *and* Advancing Small Colleges

Few things are more enjoyable than witnessing men and women who become matched to the right mountain. It is truly a privilege to gather support for a worthy cause, and Mark Dillon's *Field Guide* celebrates both people and process. This is an important book about noble work.

—ANDREW K. BENTON
President, Pepperdine University

I am thrilled that Dr. Mark Dillon has put his thoughts about stewardship into book form. For years I have been telling people that his work at Wheaton College sets the gold standard in Christ-centered advancement work. I see this as the fruit of his own experience of generous giving, his formal theological training, and his many years of practical experience in philanthropy. His intentionality about trusting in God's provision through prayer and treating every relationship as an opportunity for ministry shines through clearly in *Giving and Getting in the Kingdom*—a book that will strengthen the work of any church or Christian ministry.

—PHILIP RYKEN
President, Wheaton College

Mark Dillon throws a lifeline to those who are struggling with securing gifts for faith-based nonprofits. He skillfully connects you with resource-raising principles he honed over his successful career at Wheaton College. *Giving and Getting in the Kingdom* is a powerful resource that will recharge your passion for stewardship!

—DAN BUSBY
President, Evangelical Council for Financial Accountability

The development of funds is most often seen as a means to serve a nobler end. Mark's book turns this conception on its head to reveal the deeper meaning and purpose God envisions for both giver and steward of gifts. There is no better voice to bring clarity to the calling of advancing Christ's kingdom than my friend Mark Dillon.

—DAN COATS
United States Senator

Mark Dillon's *Giving and Getting in the Kingdom* integrates the concerns of faith and philanthropy in the way that Christian educators have long talked about integrating faith and learning. While philanthropy within the Christian context must be professionally sound by any standard, it must go beyond simply being good philanthropy if it is to meet the standards of God's kingdom. Dillon invites the reader to consider a truly Christian approach to philanthropy—one grounded first in a theological vision of God the Giver, and then lived out in both fundraisers and donors as they respond naturally to God's gifts through the faithful and transforming practices of stewardship and gratitude.

—SHIRLEY A. MULLEN
President, Houghton College

Raising funds for the ministry is not always seen as a win-win proposition on the part of the giver and the getter. Through this field guide, Mark Dillon effectively shows how parting with your money can truly be a joy to the giver as well as to those responsible for getting it. In my opinion, Mark Dillon is one of the leading visionaries in this area of kingdom work. Follow his advice and you will achieve the best practices for your church or parachurch organization.

—PHIL HUBBARD
President, Hubbard Management Group, LLC, Chairman, English Language Institute in China

Mark Dillon practices what he preaches. He is kingdom-minded and profoundly effective in his work. It has been a privilege for me to partner with him over the past ten years in encouraging givers to give generously to build God's kingdom. I highly commend his thoughtful and practical book for those interested in serving givers well and resourcing causes abundantly.

—TODD HARPER
President, Generous Giving

GIVING & GETTING IN THE KINGDOM

IN THE KINGDOM

— a field guide —

R. Mark Dillon, Ph.D.

MOODY PUBLISHERS

CHICAGO

All Scripture quotations, unless otherwise indicated, are taken from the *Holy Bible, New International Version*®, NIV®. Copyright ©1973, 1978, 1984 by Biblica, Inc.™ Used by permission of Zondervan. All rights reserved worldwide.

All websites and phone numbers listed herein are accurate at the time of publication, but may change in the future or cease to exist. The listing of website references and resources does not imply publisher endorsement of the site's entire contents. Groups and organizations are listed for informational purposes, and listing does not imply publisher endorsement of their activities.

Published in association with the literary agency of Mark Sweeney & Associates, Bonita Springs, Florida 34135.

Editor: Brandon O'Brien

Cover Design: Mary Leiser

Cover Image: 02-07-10 © Tibor Nagy iStock

Interior design: Smartt Guys design

ISBN: 978-0-8024-0592-0

We hope you enjoy this book from Moody Publishers. Our goal is to provide high-quality, thought-provoking books and products that connect truth to your real needs and challenges. For more information on other books and products written and produced from a biblical perspective, go to www.moodypublishers.com or write to:

Moody Publishers
820 N. LaSalle Boulevard
Chicago, IL 60610

1 3 5 7 9 10 8 6 4 2

Printed in the United States of America

To Don Meyer and David Dunlop
By the excellence of their example,
they have been my True North in giving and getting.

CONTENTS

FOREWORD

I've read a lot of books on fundraising. I believe I've read just about all of them. Mark Dillon's new book stands alone.

Let me tell you what I like most about it. It is replete with real-life stories of those he has met during his quarter century in the field. And stories are the most effective way to provide a powerful lesson. But that's not all.

Mark writes about the joy of giving and makes it come alive. But that's not all.

The book abounds with personal stories that have an indelible impact. It's obvious that for Mark, fundraising is his ministry. But that's not all.

I'll tell you what makes the difference. Mark shows a clear pathway for giving and getting for the kingdom. All of the signposts are in place. Even though the book is about fundraising—and any professional would benefit from reading it—you feel the presence of Jesus throughout. Investing in the kingdom is serious business. But Mark also makes it a joyous journey.

To the Christian, giving is not an option. Mark Dillon shows us how to make this come alive. The book sings and soars. Among the small handful of volumes in our field I consider outstanding, this book is first among equals.

Jerold Panas

Executive Partner, Jerold Panas, Linzy & Partners

INTRODUCTION

The kingdom of heaven is like a merchant looking for
fine pearls. When he found one of great value, he went away
and sold everything he had and bought it.

—Matthew 13:45–46

The kingdom of God is the realm and reign of God, through Christ, over all who have received His redemption and forgiveness of sin (Colossians 1:13–14). Therefore, the eternal kingdom is the true home of every child of God. For them it is: a precious gift (*take your inheritance, the kingdom prepared for you since the creation of the world*); an earnest prayer (*Thy kingdom come*); a present experience (*the kingdom of God is within you*); a growing reality (*the kingdom of God is like yeast*); a future hope (*live lives worthy of God, who calls you into His kingdom and glory*); and an eternal inheritance (*we are receiving a kingdom that cannot be shaken*).

> GOD IS PLEASED TO USE INTENTIONAL, AUTHENTIC RELATIONSHIPS, THE FAITHFUL CALLING OF GOD'S PEOPLE TO GIVE, AND OBEDIENCE TO A BIBLICAL VIEW OF RESOURCES TO ADVANCE HIS ETERNAL KINGDOM.

All of life, then, takes place within the reign of God. This is true even in the matter of giving and getting resources for doing God's work in this world. God is pleased to use intentional, authentic relationships, the faithful calling of God's people to give, and obedience to a biblical view of resources to advance His eternal kingdom. Therefore, giving and getting in the kingdom should differ in appearance and purpose from what the world knows as philanthropy and fundraising. This is not to say that giving and getting outside the kingdom is without merit; (philanthropy *does* matter) and, of course, doing so within the kingdom is no assurance of eternal value (not every gift given or dollar spent, even with good intentions to advance Christ's kingdom, is necessarily honorable in God's sight). Nonetheless, the thoughtful giver and the thoughtful gatherer of resources within God's kingdom operate on a level of eternal significance. That is what this book is about.

In this world, money fuels ministry. Everyone can agree on that. Even the street preacher must get transportation to the place of ministry, basic training and equipment for the doing of ministry, a way home, and a place to call home. It is just as true for the multimillion dollar, multinational relief agency. And it is a present reality for the local congregation, the Christian college, the homeless shelter, and the mission agency.

So the option is not money for ministry or not. It is the choice between a thoughtful, biblically consistent, and productive approach to giving and getting in the kingdom on the one hand and a poorly informed or downright misguided approach to seeking fuel for ministry on the other. The premise of this book is that the challenge of the times and the eternal importance of the task require the former. Any lesser effort does not match the excellence that service in Christ's kingdom requires.

Giving and Getting in the Kingdom focuses on who we are and how we approach the matter of giving and getting resources for Christian ministry. While serving as a comprehensive guide to the essentials of raising money for worthy causes, this book also examines why people give and explores the role of fundraiser as a high calling and worthy vocation for a pastor, president, trustee, director, development professional, or motivated volunteer.

An important word about "getting." Getting is not *taking*. Getting is not talking someone out of money they don't want to give. Rather, getting (or gathering—we will use these terms interchangeably) is the process of calling men and women to be rich toward God with their resources. Getting resources for ministry is not merely to enrich a particular organization. At its best, getting is for the sake of the kingdom and promotes the Christian steward's own service to the Lord Jesus Christ.

> GETTING IS NOT TALKING SOMEONE OUT OF MONEY THEY DON'T WANT TO GIVE.

This book is not about how to build a program or ways to raise more money, although God may use its application to accomplish both. Rather, it will be a source for the serious fundraiser to turn to again and again to ground, focus, and reconnect to the fundamental values that separate the salesperson from the true friend, those who live *off* philanthropy from those who live *for* philanthropy. This book will help pastors, presidents, ministry leaders, board members, new development officers, and other staff in the nonprofit sector gain understanding and perspective on true giving and principled getting that will strengthen their capacity and potential to adequately fund their important missions. It will also assist the thoughtful Christian giver in what is a more difficult task than many realize: giving well.

To ground ourselves for the fundraising task, we must first look at giving from God's perspective. How is giving consistent with God's very nature? How does God's nature inform the fundraising task? That grounding provides the context for us to understand philanthropy (literally, "love of mankind") from a biblical point of view. This will allow us to consider the permutations of American philanthropy, both historically and in the present, and discern what stands up to a kingdom point of view and what falls short.

With the groundwork set, we will examine the mind (and heart) of the giver. What motivates giving and why? Are all givers the same, or do they fall into distinct categories? How does understanding the heart of the donor inform the fundraising task? How does the fundraiser influence the heart of the donor?

Fundamental to our thinking about giving and getting is to understand how money flows: who has it, who does not, and how that may affect the obligation to give or the appeal to get.

With a grasp of why people give, we turn to the matter of *getting* in the kingdom. How can a ministry—a representative of that ministry—honor Christ and His people in the process of seeking God's money, from God's people, for God's work? Is our method merely the commonly accepted approach with verbiage that makes it "Christian," or is there a way of getting that is consistent with kingdom values? What practices are common to all fundraising efforts? What is profoundly different in the Christian context? Is there a common approach to everyone, or does fundraising for ministry call for a level of care that is radical and individualized?

> OPTING OUT IS NOT AN OPTION. THERE IS ONLY GOOD FUNDRAISING OR BAD.

Finally, what does Christian fundraising look like in real life? How does a church or any explicitly Christian organization operate to adequately fund its mission transparently and effectively? What does it mean for the board? What are the implications for the president, chief executive officer, or pastor? How does principled fundraising mark the priorities and activities of the staff and leadership responsible for securing resources? How does authentic engagement by the supporting constituency of the ministry affect the outcomes for the ministry and the kingdom?

In the matter of giving and getting in Christian ministry, opting out is not an option. There is only good fundraising or bad—

thoughtful stewardship or haphazard—and there are a frightful number of ill-informed, inadequate, and unworthy attitudes about and approaches to giving and getting in the kingdom. God does use intentionality about the matter of giving to move us to joyful service in His eternal kingdom. Let's journey together to understand and apply principles that are not only effective but honoring to the One in whose kingdom we are called to serve.

PART I

GIVING IN THE KINGDOM: A WAY OF THINKING

Do not take it, therefore, as an undoing, to lay up treasures in heaven, though you leave yourselves but little on earth. You lose no great advantage for heaven by becoming poor—in pursuing one's way, the lighter you travel, the better.

—**RICHARD BAXTER** from *The Reformed Pastor*

Pilgrims travel light.

—**RANDY ALCORN**

CHAPTER

1

GOD CREATED US
TO **GIVE**

See that you also excel in this grace of giving.

—2 Corinthians 8:7

The Christian faith rests on this fundamental truth: God, in Christ, gave once and for all the most perfect and unmerited gift in all of history—redemption of sin and a "living hope" of eternal life through the death and resurrection to life of Jesus Christ from the dead (1 Peter 1:3-4). It is not possible to fully understand giving and getting in the kingdom until we see the God who gives as revealed in Holy Scripture. Giving is fundamental to God's nature, and grace is at the core of true giving. God's gracious gift gives context and meaning to *our* impulse to give and helps explain the joy that comes from the act of giving. God's gift of breath and eternal life naturally impels us to give with gratitude to Him. God's activity on our behalf, and our response to it, is the key to unlocking the unique character of giving in the kingdom.

GOD IS A GIVER

The witness of Holy Scripture and God's creation resoundingly affirms that God is a God who gives. It is in His very nature. It defines

His character.

The creation of the world was a gift. Entrusting His creation to mankind was a gift. His forbearance with a sinful and recalcitrant human race is a gift. His provision, in Christ, for deliverance from the bondage of sin to sanctification and hope was the greatest gift. It is no wonder, then, that humankind, the creatures of the God who gives, would have the impulse to give hardwired into our beings.

GRACE IS AT THE CORE OF TRUE GIVING

While any gift is an event—even a transaction—it is, at its best, rooted in a most beautiful word: grace. Grace has been well-defined as unmerited favor. Grace is the oxygen that gives life and breath to living—and to giving in the kingdom. God's common grace certainly extends to all of creation. The prophet Isaiah declared that "grace is shown to the wicked" (Isaiah 26:10) and the New Testament affirms, "For since the creation of the world, God's invisible qualities—his eternal power and divine nature—have been clearly seen, being understood from what has been made" (Romans 1:20). But, in a most particular way, God has extended saving grace to those who inhabit His kingdom through the gift of eternal life through Christ. Grace, of course, is a central theme of the Bible, and a key to understanding life in the kingdom. The Scripture passages below give a taste of the centrality of grace in God's interaction with His creation:

- The Lord is gracious and righteous; our God is full of compassion. (Psalm 116:5)
- We have peace with God through our Lord Jesus Christ, through whom we have gained access by faith into this grace in which we now stand. (Romans 5:1b–2)
- If you, O Lord, kept a record of sins, O Lord, who could stand? (Psalm 130:3)

- And God raised us up with Christ and seated us with him in the heavenly realms in Christ Jesus, in order that in the coming ages he might show the incomparable riches of his grace, experienced in his kindness to us in Christ Jesus. (Ephesians 2:6–7)
- So too, at the present time there is a remnant chosen by grace. And if by grace, then it is no longer by works; if it were, grace would no longer be grace. (Romans 11:5–6)

Life and breath are a gift of the Creator. So is the grace in which inhabitants of His kingdom stand. It is incongruous, then, to have any response to this lavish, unmerited gift than the strong impulse to give back.

GIVING IS OUR RESPONSE TO GOD'S GIFT

If our Creator's very nature is to give, and if His giving nature has been amply demonstrated by His grace extended to us in Christ, then we have both an explanation and an imperative for giving in the kingdom. No aspect of life is a more natural reciprocation for God's gifts to us than giving.

The impulse to "give back" is imbedded in the human heart (see chapter 15 on Reciprocity, p.209). It is fundamental to all kinds of giving, both within and outside the kingdom. But within the kingdom, giving away time and resources, at its best, is in grateful response to God's indescribable gift in Christ. The thoughtful Christian steward reflects the sentiment of Scripture: "the grace of God teaches us to . . . live . . . godly lives in this present age, while we wait for the blessed hope" (Titus 2:11–13). "Each one should use whatever gift he has received to serve others, faithfully administering God's grace in its various forms" (1 Peter 4:10). "However, I consider my life worth nothing to me, if only I may finish the race and complete the task the Lord Jesus has given me—the task of testifying to the gospel of God's grace" (Acts 20:24).

For anyone, giving back—in response to a kind gesture, or an education received, or in response to help in the midst of a dire situation—is both a natural human impulse and a noble gesture. In the kingdom, however, there is a divine obligation for those who have been recipients of God's grace in Christ to give away time, talent, and treasure: to the poor, to widows and orphans, to Christ's church, and to every conceivable person or program that advances His eternal kingdom. However, as we will see, that "obligation" is often accompanied by great joy, rendering that obligation an easy "burden."

For inhabitants of Christ's kingdom, giving is far from a point of pride or distinction. Rather, it is a privilege granted to citizens of the kingdom. That is one reason that human recognition of a gift to the kingdom is so tricky (see chapter 15). Giving out of the context of the grace we have received is not, ultimately, an idea we thought up. It is a grateful *response* to a lavish gift. But as we will see, this divine obligation and impulse to give is not a heavy burden to bear or a mere duty to perform, but is pure joy.

GIVING BRINGS JOY

It stands to reason that Christians who give in response to God's grace in their lives experience deep joy and satisfaction. Scripture is replete with references to the joy and blessing that comes from a generous spirit.

- Blessed is he who has regard for the weak; the Lord delivers him in times of trouble. (Psalm 41:1)
- Good will come to him who is generous and lends freely, who conducts his affairs with justice. (Psalm 112:5)
- One man gives freely, yet gains even more; another withholds unduly, but comes to poverty. (Proverbs 11:24)
- A generous man will prosper; he who refreshes others will himself be refreshed. (Proverbs 11:25)

- Command them to do good, to be rich in good deeds, and to be generous and willing to share. (1 Timothy 6:18)

- For I testify that they gave as much as they were able, and even beyond their ability. Entirely on their own, they urgently pleaded with us for the privilege of sharing in this service to the saints. (2 Corinthians 8:3–4)

Notice the strong correlation between generosity and joy. The amount of the gift itself is irrelevant. A million-dollar gift can be joyless, just as the widow's mite can be cause for much admiration and joy (Mark 12:41–43). What does it mean to give generously? I once heard Warren Buffet say in an interview (I paraphrase here) in reflection upon his gift of $26 *billion*, "My gift has not changed my lifestyle one bit. I still go to the movies I want to go to and eat at the restaurants I care to dine at." He went on to say, "What about the person who gives a gift that requires that they can't go to the movies or eat out? They are the true givers—the true heroes (of philanthropy)." Mr. Buffet's observation is right on the money. The size of the gift does not define generosity. Rather, generosity might well be defined as giving to the extent that it alters our choices and activities.

> THE SIZE OF THE GIFT DOES NOT DEFINE GENEROSITY.

Randy Alcorn, in his marvelous book *The Treasure Principle*, gives a powerful visual illustration of the proper worldview of a follower of Christ.[1] It is simply this:

●————————————————————————————

The dot represents this life—a mere blip on the screen in terms of eternity. The solid line represents the expanse of eternity. Life on this earth is a tiny slice of the eternal existence of Christ's kingdom.

The immediacy of our lives, complicated greatly by our sinful tendency to look out for our interests above all others, causes us to put far too many resources in the dot (the matters of this world) and fewer investments in the line (the eternal kingdom). True givers in the kingdom, recipients of God's lavish grace, joyfully invest in people and programs that will outlast the dot. And invariably, those who invest generously in Christ's kingdom bear out the truth of Scripture: "For the kingdom of God is not a matter of eating and drinking, but of righteousness, peace, and joy" (Romans 14:17). Giving, at its best, is not a self-motivated act of philanthropy but a joyful response to a prior gift—the grace of God in Christ.

> GIVING, AT ITS BEST, IS NOT A SELF-MOTIVATED ACT OF PHILANTHROPY BUT A JOYFUL RESPONSE TO A PRIOR GIFT—THE GRACE OF GOD IN CHRIST.

That certainly distinguishes giving in the kingdom from what is commonly understood by the term "philanthropy." Nonetheless, philanthropy, that impulse to love and care for others, is within every human heart. And giving in the kingdom is not well-understood until we grasp the world of philanthropy.

CHAPTER 2

PHILANTHROPY
AND THE **KINGDOM**

---

*He who governed the world before I was born shall
take care of it likewise when I am dead.
My part is to improve the present moment.*
—John Wesley

AN AMERICAN DISTINCTIVE

The world in which we engage in giving and getting (and here I am talking primarily about the United States) is not without history and context. Whether we know it or not, and whether we acknowledge it or not, the American philanthropic tradition is the ocean in which we have grown up and in which we operate. It would be foolish to think about giving in the kingdom without understanding the uniqueness and pervasiveness of American philanthropy.

Philanthropy, literally, "love of mankind," has been called America's most distinctive virtue, and it is difficult to argue otherwise. Economist Walter Williams claims that 80 percent of privately contributed gifts in all of human history have been donated by US citizens. There is no nation on earth whose people have freely given back a greater amount of their earned wealth for the welfare of their fellow citizens than the United States. This is not a statement from

THE INFLUENCE OF RELIGION, AND PARTICULARLY CHRISTIANITY, CAN EASILY BE TRACED TO THE EARLIEST SETTLERS OF THE NEW WORLD.

national conceit; it is a verity that is beyond dispute and freely acknowledged throughout the world. But what is it about American society that has made this so?

There seems to be consensus in the literature that America's philanthropic spirit has been, and continues to be, fueled by three converging forces: the prominence of religion, the penchant for creating voluntary associations to meet human needs, and the broad creation of wealth throughout a democratic republic. It is well worth a little time to consider the forces that influence giving in America. By doing so, we will better understand giving in general as well as the forces that continue to shape giving in the kingdom.

RELIGION MOTIVATES PHILANTHROPY

Any reading of current giving in America reveals that over half of all individual giving (over $150 billion in a recent year) goes into the collection plates of churches or are credited to the accounts of church-related hospitals, schools, and social service agencies. Beyond that, churches mobilize millions of volunteers each year. The influence of religion, and particularly Christianity, can easily be traced to the earliest settlers of the New World. John Winthrop, in 1630, preached the famous sermon, "A Model of Christian Charity," on board a ship from Old England to New England. In it, Winthrop said, "In this duty of love we must love brotherly without dissimulation, we must love one another with a pure heart fervently, we must bear one another's burdens, we must not look only on our own things, but also on the things of our brethren. Neither must we think that the Lord will bear with such failings at our hands as he doth from those among whom we have lived . . . "[2]

It is beyond our scope to dwell on the link between religion and philanthropy in America, but even a cursory study reveals early giants like John Winthrop, William Penn, Cotton Mather, and George Whitefield taking leading roles in linking love of mankind, the Christian imperative to love our neighbor, into the hearts and minds of early Americans. Cotton Mather (1663–1728) implored all who would listen, "Let us try to do good with as much application of mind as wicked men employ in doing evil." He was quick to add, "Charity to the souls of men is the highest form of giving."[3] William Penn said that, "The best recreation is to do good." There would be time for enjoyment when "the pale faces are more commiserated, the pinched bellies relieved and the naked backs clothed, when the famished poor, the distressed widow, and the helpless orphan . . . are provided for."[4] George Whitefield (1714–1770) is known as one of the great preachers and a central figure of the Great Awakening. Lesser known was his ardent support to establish an orphanage in the colony

> REGULAR CHURCH/ SYNAGOGUE ATTENDANCE REMAINS THE SINGLE GREATEST PREDICTOR OF GIVING AND VOLUNTEERING.

of Georgia, as well as his securing books and financial assistance for (once!) struggling colleges: Harvard, Dartmouth, Princeton, and the University of Pennsylvania.

Of course, there were certainly secular strains of philanthropy in early America.

Ben Franklin is a prominent example, and Andrew Carnegie is the classic nineteenth-century example. Nonetheless, the imperatives of the Christian gospel propelled a great deal of philanthropy, leaving a mark on the DNA of the young nation, and flourishing today, even in a very different cultural environment. Even today, 91 percent of Americans report belief in God. And regular church/synagogue attendance remains the single greatest predictor of giving and volunteering. The ethos of faith and the noble obligation to "give back" is alive and well, even in an increasingly pluralistic culture.

VOLUNTARY ASSOCIATION NOURISHES
PHILANTHROPY

Alexis de Tocqueville was a French nobleman who came to America barely fifty years after its founding. He and his friend Gustave de Beaumont traveled throughout the new republic, seeking a cohesive explanation of American democracy. His monumental book, *Democracy in America*, was published in 1835. A foundational observation about the American people is captured in this passage: "Americans of all ages, all conditions, and all dispositions constantly form associations. . . . Wherever at the head of a great undertaking you see the government in France, or a man of rank in England, in the United States you will be sure to find an association."[5]

The powerful combination of freedom of assembly and (largely) Christian charity propelled Americans to volunteer, whether to help the less fortunate or to provide services that the young government was unable or unwilling to provide. Whether to advance a political cause or to start a business, Os Guinness aptly notes that, "Freedom of association (in America) correlates to freedom of conscience. The voluntary church, with its voluntary membership and voluntary contributions, is the historical prototype of the voluntary association."[6]

The acknowledged dean of the study of philanthropy, Robert Payton, has defined philanthropy simply as, "voluntary action for the public good."[7] This definition holds up well in thinking about philanthropy, whether religiously motivated or not. James Douglas, in his book *Why Charity?*, makes the brilliant point that philanthropy is the instrument that societies have used to compensate for the indifference of the marketplace and the incompetence of the state. The shortcomings of market economies and provisions by the state are why acts of compassion in community will always be needed in all societies. Of course, while compassion in community is found in many other nations and cultural contexts, it is undeniably prevalent and deeply rooted in American culture. Few would question that the heavy Christian influence on early America gave rise to its global reputation as a giving nation.

WEALTH CREATION FUELS PHILANTHROPY

It may be more than coincidental that 1776 marked the birth of the United States and the publication of *The Wealth of Nations,* by Adam Smith. It is not difficult to link the rise of a republic with the broader rise of wealth made possible by a constitution that valued freedom and opportunity.

Robert Payton has said, "Philanthropy occurs at the juncture of economics and religion."[8] He also notes that "the philanthropic tradition is deeply rooted in religion in America. (It is) the most powerful motive force behind individual charity."[9] He has observed that America's philanthropic tradition flows from two streams: "charity —acts of mercy to relieve the suffering of the innocent and helpless; and philanthropy—acts of community to improve the quality of life."[10] The Industrial Revolution, while arguably creating as many opportunities for philanthropic effort as wealth from which to give, continued the process of wealth creation throughout the nation. This broad swath of relative wealth and the ethos of abundance, coupled with religious roots and the penchant for voluntary associations, solidified the giving spirit and activity of America.

This brief overview must not leave the overall impression that the people of the United States are the only compassionate, giving people on earth! And, in fact, if the country lauded in the world as the most generous nation on earth truly gives less than 3 percent of its GNP away, there is plenty of room for modesty. Nonetheless, to effectively engage in giving and getting for the kingdom, particularly in the United States, it is important to understand the history and context from which Americans give (and get) today.

PHILANTHROPY,
ROOTED IN **CHRIST,** IS
ETERNALLY **SIGNIFICANT**

Thanks be to God for his indescribable gift!
—2 Corinthians 9:15

Philanthropy, wherever it is found, is driven by a conviction that any Christ-follower would affirm: the dignity and worth of every individual. That is what impels, for example, Bill and Melinda Gates to give away a staggering $28 *billion* of their wealth, primarily to provide health care and education to underserved and underprivileged people in the United States and around the world.

Tangible assistance to those who could not live or hope to prosper without it is what drives the Gates and Warren Buffet to issue the challenge to the world's billionaires (there are over a thousand of them) to pledge to give away over 50 percent of their wealth. More than sixty-nine have pledged publicly to do so (givingpledge.org)—a remarkable demonstration of love for mankind.

Yet despite this significant outpouring of tangible assistance, the efforts fall short in a significant way. How could this be? Their philanthropy is directed at genuine human need. It is generous. It is given with love and compassion and selflessness and is changing lives for the better. Philanthropy without the vertical goal of drawing people to God Himself is not without value or purpose. It certainly bears the mark of God's common grace to people of all nations and circumstances. The psalmist declares: "The Lord is good to all; he has compassion on all he has made" (Psalm 145:9).

But from a Christian perspective, care for the temporal body apart from care for the soul, which we know to be eternal, falls short. Surely followers of Christ are to care for human needs. The book of Proverbs sounds the theme that is replete in the Bible: "He who is kind to the poor lends to the Lord, and he will reward him for what he has done" (19:17); "The righteous care about justice for the poor, but the wicked have no such concern" (29:7); and, "Speak up for those who cannot speak for themselves" (31:8). It is no less an imperative of the Christian than of any human being to care for the poor. But Jesus Himself said, "Do not be afraid of those who kill the body but cannot kill the soul. Rather, be afraid of the one who can destroy both soul and body in hell" (Matthew 10:28). The King of heaven declared the eternal soul to be of greater consequence than the temporal body. So should His followers. In the kingdom, love of mankind cannot be fully realized by relieving suffering or extending opportunity alone. In the kingdom, philanthropy is temporal *and* eternal. It is about this world, to be sure, but it must have in mind the eternal destiny of the soul (not just the "dot" but the "line" as well). The reach of secular philanthropy is commendable and may even advance God's purposes in this world. But in the larger context of the kingdom, it falls short. The ultimate form of charity is to share the gospel, and kingdom philanthropy furthers this end whether directly or indirectly.

So how does the Christian church approach giving and getting? A two-thousand-year history is beyond the scope of this book, but we can look at the past century and a half of giving and getting in

> IN THE KINGDOM, PHILANTHROPY IS TEMPORAL *AND* ETERNAL.

the church to provide an important context to the current state of things in this important realm. There are two prevailing attitudes about how God makes financial provision for ministry, and they are well illustrated by two giants of the nineteenth-century Christian church, George Mueller and D. L. Moody.

MUELLER'S VIEW OF GETTING

George Mueller was born in Germany, and converted to Christianity at the age of twenty. Soon after, in 1829, he moved to London to engage in missionary work. By 1832, he moved to Bristol, England, where he initially pastored a congregation, then established the ministry for which he is famous, an orphanage.

As a matter of principle, Mueller steadfastly refused to speak of needs, relying rather on earnest prayer among friends and supporters. While he would share examples of God's marvelous provision of specific needs in times past, he would not share current needs. The stories of remarkable provisions, often at the very last critical moment of need, became well known and revered. Dr. A. T. Pierson was the guest of George Mueller at his orphanage. He says:

> One night when all the household had retired, he [Mueller] asked Pierson to join him in prayer. He told him that there was absolutely nothing in the house for next morning's breakfast. My friend tried to remonstrate with him and to remind him that all the stores were closed. Mueller knew all that. He had prayed as he always prayed, and he never told anyone of his needs but God. They prayed—at least Mueller did—and Pierson tried to. They went to bed and slept, and breakfast *for two thousand children was there in abundance at the usual breakfast hour.* Neither Mueller nor Pierson ever knew how the answer came. The story was told next morning to Simon Short of Bristol, under pledge of secrecy until the benefactor died. The details of it are thrilling, but all

that need be told here is that the Lord called him out of bed in the middle of the night to send breakfast to Mueller's orphanage, and knowing nothing of the need, or of the two men at prayer, he sent provisions that would feed them a month.[11]

J. Hudson Taylor and Amy Carmichael adopted Mueller's approach in funding their missionary enterprises, further establishing a pattern that was admired and adopted in evangelical outreach. Well into the first half of the twentieth century, several foreign mission agencies, such as the African Inland Mission and the Latin America Mission, adhered to the pattern of refusing to publicize the needs of missionaries. This approach, while mostly abandoned in the realm of Christian ministry today, continues to live on in the minds of many as the more spiritual approach to getting resources for ministry, both in the church and in Christian-based endeavors.

MOODY'S VIEW OF GETTING

In roughly the same era, but on a different continent, another convert to Christianity, D. L. Moody, sought to establish a foothold for the gospel and the societal needs all around him. However, his approach was decidedly different from that of George Mueller. Moody was a product of the rough-and-tumble of the marketplace.

Michael Hamilton, in *More Money, More Ministry,* aptly describes Moody's contribution to getting money for ministry. "The pioneering characteristic of Moody the businessman is that he was, in every respect of the word, an entrepreneur. He developed a vision for innovative methods of evangelization, laid plans to carry out the vision, and then sold the vision to backers and workers. He thus marshaled resources, financial and human, into independent organizations that would produce the religious product—be it education, publications, or revivals—that would embody the vision."[12]

Moody exemplified the American entrepreneurial spirit: identify a need, establish a plan to meet that need, enlist financial support to carry out the plan, and demonstrate to "investors" the worthiness of their investment. Quite an abrupt departure from Mueller's refusal to ask for gifts or even to make needs known!

ARE THEY COMPATIBLE?

Here are two fundamental approaches to getting in God's kingdom: quiet, fervent, prayerful reliance on God's provision for ministry and the more entrepreneurial/business model of identifying a need, establishing a plan to remedy that need, and seeking and urging investors to meet that need. Anyone who lives in or observes the Christian church knows that George Mueller's approach to money for ministry—whether or not his name is familiar—lives on in the minds and hearts of twenty-first-century Christians. There is something guileless and winsome and intuitive about utter dependence upon God for financial resources. It seems sublime to never talk about needs and to ignore the impulse to even ask. Moreover, there is something somewhat repellent about money for ministry that is gained by a more common approach of planning and asking and implementing, only to plan, ask, and implement again!

It must be said, however, that Mueller's approach avoids challenging God's people toward their responsibility to allocate their resources, time, talent, and treasure to the work of God in this world (something we will return to often in this book). The question is, then, are the approaches of Mueller and Moody mutually exclusive, or is it possible to blend the two? Can a careful, thoughtful plan, persuasively presented with passion and conviction, be compatible with utter dependence upon Christ, both in framing and seeking funds for the plan? Perhaps there is a third way to think about getting resources for ministry that is utterly dependent upon God's provision while still calling God's people to participate in His activity in His world.

This third way can be illustrated with another historical example.

A rough contemporary of Mueller and Moody was a man named Charles Blanchard. I know of him because he is a key figure in the history of the college I serve, Wheaton College. Charles was the second president of Wheaton College, and occupied that role for a remarkable forty-three years, from 1882–1925.

Dr. Blanchard traveled far and wide to raise money for this small, fledgling college on the prairie of Illinois, dedicated to classic education in the Christian tradition for the transformation of society in service to Christ's kingdom. The future of the college was far from secure. So he visited individuals throughout the Midwest and extending to the East Coast. His diaries reveal that he met with some of the most prominent industrialists and financial magnates of his time—Philip S. Armour, Henry Field, W. H. Wanamaker, George M. Pullman, C. H. McCormick, and J. P. Morgan—as well as scores of lesser-known individuals with the capacity to advance his college.

A visit to the Wheaton College Archives and Special Collections reveals at least a dozen leather diaries kept by President Blanchard. Inside, in Dr. Blanchard's meticulous handwriting, are detailed records of visits completed, specific asks made, responses to solicitations, and brief notes about future actions.

The diaries reveal hundreds of comments, pledges, and responses that any seasoned fundraiser would recognize: "Can't now. Perhaps in the spring." "Perhaps later." "Finally declines, but in very kind tone." "100 dollars, if I can, in June." "Don't believe in Christian education." "I'm a lawyer, go see the capitalists." "Never subscribes (pledges). Don't believe in subscriptions." "We are a corporation, we have no soul."

But inside the front cover of one of his diaries, Charles Blanchard inscribed two perpetual reminders that saturated his efforts: "And my God will meet all your needs according to his glorious riches in Christ Jesus" (Philippians 4:19) and "Ask and it will be given to you;

seek and you will find; knock and the door will be opened to you" (Matthew 7:7).

The premise of this book is that God does honor the ministry that is thoughtful and relevant and winsomely articulates its cause. Far from being a point of self-satisfaction, pride, or self-sufficiency, the results of the ministry and the funding provided for the ministry can be confidently attributed to the grace of God in Christ. After all, who provided the mind and heart to meet the need? Who planted the desire to build Christ's kingdom? Who gave the courage to ask? Who granted the ability to earn the resources and the desire to release them for the sake of the kingdom? It is God and God alone.

> GOD DOES HONOR THE MINISTRY THAT IS THOUGHTFUL AND RELEVANT AND WINSOMELY ARTICULATES ITS CAUSE.

Let me suggest a guiding principle in the matter of getting for the kingdom. Remember the words of the apostle Paul to the believers at Corinth. They were struggling with whom to credit as the authority in their church. Was it Apollos? Paul? Someone else? The powerful word to the church was this: "I planted the seed, Apollos watered it, but God made it grow" (1 Corinthians 3:6).

While the context of Paul's word to the Corinthians was the matter of evangelism, the wider application to the task of gathering resources holds. At the end of the day, the CEO can say, "It was my vision." The board can say, "We stepped forward with the key decisions." The fundraiser can say, "I worked with the key donors and asked for the gifts." The key donor can say, "Without my gift, this never would have happened." The architect can say, "I designed a functional building." But in the delicate matter of giving and getting in the kingdom, there is one reality that sweeps the others away in importance: "It was God, not we, who made it happen!"

This is radically different from mere fundraising and stands apart from philanthropy as it is commonly known. To give and get in the kingdom is to see God in, under, and through every aspect of the process. The danger of Mueller's approach is that what seems to be childlike faith in God for His provision may be missing an opportunity to call God's people to obedience and generosity. The inherent danger in creating a vision and boldly calling God's people to fund it, as in Moody's approach, is the human tendency to stray from discerning God's leading into merely fulfilling personal or corporate ambition and perhaps missing the elements of dependent prayer and humble gratitude. The fervent goal of every Christian endeavor to secure gifts must begin with, abide in, and culminate in honoring God alone as the One who makes it grow.

CHAPTER

THE MIND OF THE GIVER

*To give money away is an easy matter and in
any man's power. But to decide to whom to give it, and
how large and when, and for what purpose and how,
is neither in every man's power nor an easy matter.*

—Aristotle

NOT ALL GIVERS ARE THE SAME

You have carefully crafted the financial appeal in email form. It is informative and, if you do say so yourself, inspiring. It does not focus on need but opportunity. You offer specific examples of how this program is cost-effective, unique, and clearly meeting a need that closely aligns with your organization's mission. You are bold and clear in asking for a gift, and yet you appropriately express empathy for the recipient of the letter and reliance upon God to enable this particular program to go forward. The graphics are professional and compelling, but not excessive. You wait expectantly.

Three weeks later, it is time to review the responses. Your IT department verifies that of the one thousand emails sent, only 38 percent of the emails were even opened! Ugh! But what about the gifts? How many came in and what do they total? How did people respond to the appeal?

Here's an email response. It says, in part, "Thanks for your informative email. I've thought for a long time you should be doing something like this. Hope this gift of $250 helps." *Not bad*, you think, spirits lifted. *In fact, this is great.*

Then you look at response number two: "Why do you keep sending me emails begging for money? Don't I give you enough already? I've received six appeals for funds from you in the past two months. How much are all these appeals costing you, anyway?" *Yikes*, you say to yourself, *I'd better figure out what's going on there!*

Response number three: "Please call me. I have a few questions regarding how this program works. I'd like to consider an investment over the next couple of years." *Sweet!*

Then, response number four: "I wish I could give, but I'm on a fixed income and I just cannot this year. Please know that I care about your work and pray for you regularly."

Response number five: "That's it. Take me off your list. You are always asking for money, but when I wrote your CEO with a complaint last year, I didn't even get a response. Why should I care about an organization that is unresponsive to me?"

> THERE ARE AT LEAST FOUR KINDS OF GIVERS.

In total: 620 people didn't even bother to open the email, but 157 responded with gifts, totaling $18,780 dollars—not bad! But, over half who read the appeal gave *nothing*, and three people were offended by the contact and asked never to be contacted again. How can this be?

The truth is, not all givers are the same. There are at least four kinds of givers, and the more we understand about their attitudes and habits of giving, the better we can anticipate and appropriately address the mind of the donor.

THE GIFTED GIVER

It was at the dedication of a new building at the Christian college. The delight of the students and faculty was palpable. Over a hundred donors and friends had joined the joyful celebration. The building would serve many generations of students, and there was an appropriate sense of thanksgiving to God for what had been accomplished through His people.

One of the attending guests was the largest donor to the building. In fact, the building would still be a dream if not for the large and sacrificial gift he and his wife made. We would have joyfully named the facility in thanksgiving for their stewardship—but they would have none of it. Based on the way they carried themselves that day, no one would have suspected they were the primary donors to the project.

But halfway through the reception, the husband called me into one of the brand-new conference rooms. I remember thinking, *This is odd—I hope we have not done something to disappoint this remarkable couple.* Imagine my surprise when the first words out of his mouth were, "What's next?" It was immediately clear to me what he was suggesting. This project was complete. But even before the celebration was over, he wanted to know what was on the horizon for the organization that their future stewardship could influence. That is a gifted giver!

The gifted giver is rare, indeed. It is very likely that you could name the gifted givers to your organization on one or two hands, even though the gifted giver aligns most closely with the biblical examples of true givers. They may comprise only 2 to 5 percent of your givers.

The gifted giver seldom needs to be asked. As in the illustration above, the gifted giver does not need to be reminded of the obligation and joy of giving. He or she has already settled the question of joyful and abundant giving. The only remaining decision is, "To whom should I give from the resources God has entrusted to me?" For the gifted giver, giving itself is a joy and a blessing that cannot be measured. The deep satisfaction of "storing up for yourselves treasures in heaven, where moth and rust do not destroy, and where thieves do not break in and steal" (Matthew 6:20) far outstrips any fear of loss of temporal security. That deep, full joy is easily discernible by the ease with which the funds are released, and the peace that is evident in the act of giving. And giving is not out of income alone. Gifted givers often reach into their asset base—their net worth—to invest in the causes they care about. While gifted giving is normative for the disciple of Christ who seeks to live a life of obedience, its rarity is an indictment of the halfheartedness of many professing Christians.

THE THOUGHTFUL GIVER

Then there is the thoughtful giver. This category comprises far more givers in the kingdom than gifted givers. They may comprise 15 to 25 percent of givers to your organization. The thoughtful giver is profoundly aware of God's call on all of their life, possessions included. What differentiates the gifted giver from the thoughtful one is the ease with which they give of their resources. For the thoughtful giver, the pleasure of giving is tinged with a sense of obligation upon the follower of Christ. While they willingly put themselves in situations where they can be exposed to giving opportunities in the kingdom, it is often the nature of the appeal and their current circumstances that dictate whether and how much they choose to give. Giving is calibrated to current income, and rarely involves lowering their net worth to fund what they care about. They have joy in giving, to be sure, but often lack unbridled delight in investing resources for kingdom purposes. The difference from the gifted giver is a matter of degree, and it can be described as the difference between a totally open hand (the gifted giver) and the occasionally open hand of the thoughtful donor.

THE CASUAL GIVER

There is an even larger group of givers, those we will call casual givers. This group likely comprises your largest group of givers, perhaps 35 to 50 percent of them. They possess a vague understanding of their obligation to be faithful and generous stewards of their resources, but rarely seek out opportunities to give. Instead they usually give in response to a specific request. Their response to needs tends to be more out of obligation than joy. They are less likely to have had gifted giving modeled to them by family or close friends. They are more captivated by possessions and financial security than the gifted or thoughtful giver. The ask is more important to their decision than it is for more mature givers, and they often have a tendency to be wary of the solicitor and less trusting of the organization they are giving to. Their joy in giving is often tempered by the possible consequences of parting with personal possessions.

THE RELUCTANT GIVER

There is, alas, a fourth kind of giver, one we will call the reluctant giver. This may be an overly generous description, because many in this category give very little of their resources for any charitable purpose. Unfortunately, this category of giver may represent as much as a third of any congregation or constituency of a Christian organization. The reasons are multiple and complex. It could be the result of poor modeling by parents or other significant mentors. It might be the result of poor financial management in general (one whose expenses exceed their resources is not in the frame of mind or of the capacity to give). It could be a result of the poisonous (and sub-Christian) attitude that "my resources are mine, and nobody else has a claim on them." It is this group of people who are often the first to be offended by being asked for a gift, even to a very worthy cause.

If not all givers are the same, it indicates that the process of getting should be carefully adapted. A "one size fits all" approach to getting is counterproductive. How, then, should one charged with getting in the kingdom approach these distinct kinds of givers?

ENGAGING THE GIFTED GIVER

First, identify who the gifted givers are. By and large, they will not be hard to find. That is because there are so few of them and because gifted givers tend to make themselves known by their giving and their genuine interest in building Christ's kingdom through your ministry. Once identified, they are cause for thanksgiving to God. He has placed a handful of men and women in the orbit of your organization who can make a huge difference in the pursuit of your mission. Also, mature givers tend to be people of great wisdom and spiritual depth. Spending time with them will strengthen and encourage you as a faithful follower of Christ. They will also lend wisdom and direction to your organization. In short, know who they are, stay close to them, and be willing to learn from them. Consult them often. You will have uncovered a deep resource of wisdom and resources for the fulfillment of your mission.

ENGAGING THE THOUGHTFUL GIVER

First, the thoughtful givers in your orbit must be identified as well. But, they will not be as obvious to you as the gifted givers. While they may seek opportunities to invest in the kingdom, they almost certainly are investing in many other organizations: their church, human needs, and education, among others. But if the thoughtful donor does look for opportunities to invest and takes joy in their giving, it is important for those charged with getting funds for ministry to identify who they are, provide opportunities for them to hear your story, and winsomely challenge them to invest in your cause.

It is with the thoughtful givers that those responsible for getting can have the most influence—and will wisely spend the most amount of time. It is of utmost importance to identify this significant group among those who care for your cause. They are, by and large, the ones who have already given. They also tend to reach out with questions or suggestions. The thoughtful giver will be responsive to opportunities to hear the vision of your organization. But that, of course, requires that we have a coherent story to tell and an accessible venue in which to tell that story. It also requires willingness to call the thoughtful giver to action on behalf of your cause. There is genuine opportunity to move them to become gifted givers. (We will explore this in depth in Part II.)

ENGAGING THE CASUAL GIVER

The casual givers to your organization are, like the thoughtful giver, identifiable. They have likely given a gift to you in the past, or may even be current donors, although most likely at a modest level. The great opportunity with the casual giver is growing them into thoughtful or gifted givers. Any gift to your organization, whether current or the distant past, indicates a level of awareness and involvement that can be built upon. The casual giver, by definition, has at least a vague notion of their stewardship responsibility and has acted upon that at least once on behalf of your organization. That should be a great encouragement and opportunity for growth.

> THERE ARE OPPORTUNITIES TO GROW CHRISTIANS FROM RELUCTANT OR CASUAL GIVERS TO THOUGHTFUL OR GIFTED ONES.

How can a casual giver be nurtured toward becoming a thoughtful or even gifted giver? Perhaps the greatest opportunity is dialogue. Does the casual giver truly know why you exist and what ultimate value would be missing if you did not? Do they know how their gift matters to your mission? Do they remember why they gave to you in the first place? Does the reason for their lapsed or casual giving have more to do with how the organization stewarded their gift than the giver's heart toward the kingdom? Does the essence of our mission even come close to the animating passion of their stewardship? What are their own convictions about stewardship in the kingdom?

The answers to these questions might come from some sort of survey instrument but, frankly, probably require a conversation. That, of course, is painstaking work. But it is an important responsibility of those who get in the kingdom.

There is another way a casual giver can grow into a more mature giver, and that is by more fully understanding the stewardship dimensions of being a follower of Christ. The day is long past when we can assume that all who have the capacity and potential will to give to kingdom causes were taught well in their homes and in their churches. Many adults who are followers of Christ were not raised in homes with Christian values. Sadder still, many who were raised in Christian homes had poor mentoring from their parents. And many would say that the church has largely abdicated its responsibility to teach "the whole counsel of God," particularly in the area of financial stewardship.

This offers at least two opportunities for the Christian organization. Individual visits can be an important opportunity to share principles of the joy and responsibility to give to the kingdom. Interacting with casual donors about giving is a perfect opportunity to encourage donors to be "rich toward God." There are also very fine organizations such as Generous Giving (Generousgiving.org), who exist to educate and inspire Christians in radical financial giving to the kingdom. In other words, there are opportunities to grow Christians from reluctant or casual givers to thoughtful or gifted ones. Linking donors and potential donors to such resources takes the motive for encouraging generous giving away from a singular goal of meeting one organization's needs to the much more important goal of growing stewards to Christ's kingdom.

ENGAGING THE RELUCTANT GIVER

Reluctant givers are a tough group to reach, and we may be tempted to write them off as immature givers who "just don't get it." It is often this group that expresses disgust with fundraising "tactics." A veteran fundraiser I know well used to say, "Some people would simply rather be mad than give." I must confess, I've discovered that most of the people who declare, "I'm never giving another gift to your organization," have actually yet to give their *first* gift! While organizations must be careful of the time and other resources given to the task of getting in the kingdom (see chapter 6), the wise organization will seek to win and grow reluctant givers. Beyond the measures described in the previous section on winning the casual giver, the reluctant giver must be seen as one who is just as precious in the sight of God as the gifted giver—they simply have not grown to a level of maturity incumbent upon the follower of Christ. Seize every opportunity to demonstrate patience and grace, maybe not for the financial advancement of your organization but for the sake of the growth and maturity of a fellow traveler in the kingdom. It is often only through the act of giving that growth in the joy of generosity can happen.

Every organization will have gifted, thoughtful, casual, and reluctant givers or potential givers. Treating all constituents as a homogenous group might be easier, but we do so at our own peril. The more we recognize the different *kinds* of donors, and meet them at their level of need and expectation, the more worthy we will become of their support. We will have also transcended mere fundraising and helped to grow givers in God's kingdom.

GENERATIONS DIFFER

It is easy to think about givers to your organization as a monolithic group. After all, they share a common interest: you. Most likely, faith infuses their motivation for involvement. They read the same institutional magazine, view the same website, and probably receive the same mailings from the organization. But research and experience teach us that even despite these common traits, generational differences influence attitudes and giving behavior. The generational groups are fairly well known.

There is the Silent (or Builders) generation. They were born in 1945 or earlier. They comprise 39 million of the U.S. population, and an estimated 79 percent of them give at some level. Predictably, they give the largest gifts to the nonprofit sector. They plan their giving and love to be reached out to personally. They are traditional (as are most churches and nonprofits). They tend to trust the leadership and programs of well-established ministries. They are loyal to the organizations they support. Predictably, many organizations tune their messaging to focus their efforts on this group.

Then come the Boomers (born 1946–1964). They comprise a whopping 78 million of the U.S. population. An estimated 67 percent of them are givers. This huge segment of Americans is entering retirement years in large numbers, altering the landscape of housing, medical care, consumerism, and financial management in significant ways. By and large, Boomers who give do so out of a healthy sense of obligation to institutions who have nurtured them or their children. They are go-getters and are idealistic. While concerned about their resources, many are benefiting from the huge transfer of wealth from the Silent generation. This transfer of wealth makes some of the Boomers more able to give than their circumstance would indicate.

Gen Xers (1965–1980) represent 62 million of the U.S. population. It is estimated that 58 percent of them are givers, though they give in lesser amounts than their Boomer parents. Though not dismissive of organizations, philanthropy that makes a direct impact on individuals animates their giving. They are more cynical and independent than their parents. Spontaneity and ease of giving are highly valued.

Generation Y (or Millennials) were born between 1981 and 1994.

There are approximately 51 million of them, and the percentage who give to charity is very similar to Generation X. They grew up in perhaps the most child-centric generation. Maybe because of parents who showered attention and praise on them, they tend to be a self-confident group. They are good multitaskers and like to work in groups. They care about changing the world. They are networkers and like to volunteer. As a group, they are more hopeful and idealistic than Gen Xers.

Of course, individuals do not fit neatly into the "boxes" above. There are too many variables: economic, family, vocation, faith, education, and the like. But the point for giving and getting is that generations do differ. How they access information, preferences in communication, willingness and ability to volunteer, how they weigh the value of causes and organizations do differ not only from person to person but from generation to generation.

> EVERY GIVER IS THE PRODUCT OF THE SHARED EXPERIENCES OF THEIR GENERATION AND THE INDIVIDUAL INFLUENCES OF FAMILY, FAITH, AND VOCATION.

This is easily illustrated in the educational setting with alumni of the college or university. Builder and Boomer alumni will much more readily give to a general or annual fund that supports the overall program of the school. Younger alumni, in general, care more about the direct impact of their gift and are less implicitly trusting of the leadership and structures of an established institution. Older alumni more eagerly embrace the idea of a new building that will enhance campus life for generations to come. Younger alumni are far less enamored with buildings and want to know about services that will touch people directly. Mature alumni come back to campus for reunions and enjoy banquets and programs and speeches by the president. Younger alumni are impatient with programs. They appreciate their alma mater, but care more about hanging out with their classmates than rehearsing the past.

The lesson here? Every giver is the product of the shared experiences of their generation and the individual influences of family, faith, and vocation. Staying aware of those shared factors in the lives of your current and potential givers, as well as the individual influences that shape the mind and heart of the individual giver, is important to principled giving and getting. Institutions tend to homogenize communications with their constituencies. It is efficient and conserves resources. But to treat the broad generational sweep of your givers and potential givers as a captive, cohesive audience is a mistake. People and generations of people who give differ in significant ways.

> BE WISE ABOUT THE BROAD CHARACTERISTICS OF GENERATIONS, BUT DON'T JUDGE A PERSON MERELY BY THEIR AGE!

Here are a few ways to be sensitive and responsive to generations of givers. On the institutional level, make your website accessible to Builders and Boomers and relevant to Xers and Millennials. Be wise about the broad characteristics of generations, but don't judge a person merely by their age. Some Builders may prefer to receive your communications electronically and some Millennials might prefer a call or a letter to an email or text message! As much as it lies within your capabilities, let your individual discovery of a person's passions and priorities trump a categorical assumption.

Assumptions can be dangerous. Ask your givers how they want your institution and its representatives to relate to them. Ask them what is important to them. Ask them what it is about the way you conduct yourselves that de-motivates their involvement. The answers might surprise you. Of course, the goal of all this listening and interaction is not that you can change who you are to please people, but that your mission and outreach is *relevant* to those who stand ready to become more deeply supportive of your organization.

THE DONOR AS INVESTOR

We finally connected by phone after having tried for a face-to-face appointment for months. He is *that* kind of busy. He is routinely on both coasts of this country and on another continent, all in one week. The purpose of our call was to debrief on the outcomes of a very generous gift he had given over a five-year period for a very specific program. I was also hopeful that we could at least begin to talk about what might be next. What I learned on this phone call solidified what I had observed, heard, and sensed from scores of interactions with givers over the years. Most givers, most of the time, are making *investments* in the causes they support. It is part of the calculation of how much to give, when to give it, and for what to invest their capital.

We will say more about this in chapter 8 ("Put Away the Tin Cup," p.109), but many organizations that rely on individual charity fall into or perpetuate a "tin cup" mentality. The organization is poor. They have no resources of their own. They are reliant on the goodness of strangers. There is not much time for relationship building or accountability. "Just put the money in the tin cup, sir, and we'll do the best we can with it."

But my phone call revealed the heart and passion of this (and most) true giver. We reviewed the sequence of events. He had given his gift with a particular goal in mind, but was happy to allow the organization to implement as they saw fit. He asked to be updated, but did not make any unusual demands for accountability. Most of all, he had joyfully invested in an organization he loved, administered by people he trusted. We provided annual updates and what we thought to be a thorough summary of the entire program: what was accomplished, what seemed to work well, and what we would do differently. We tried to show how we would build on what had been accomplished, with or without his continued support. But I couldn't help but pick up a tinge of disappointment in his voice. I asked what was on his mind.

"In my business," he explained, "I'm involved in venture capital every day, and it's usually *my* capital. I listen to ideas and weigh whether my investment can help them achieve success. I probe for creativity and vision. I evaluate the leadership and make a judgment whether or not they have the potential to pull it off. I find ways to stay involved and in dialogue with the company along the way. I want to make sure my investment is being used as promised, and that they are as careful in managing these resources as I was in accumulating them." He went on to say, "I don't require that the venture succeeds—although I hope, of course, it does. What I'm looking for is a good attempt at a good idea. Oh, and one more thing: I really like it when those who seek my money have some 'skin in the game.' It gives me more confidence when they have committed some of their own resources to the project."

What had happened? He told me, in his gentle, gracious way, that his gift, though given freely with great love and care for the organization, was an *investment* that he wanted to make sure would pay dividends in the kingdom. We had failed to fully understand the gift as a careful investment of resources for kingdom returns. We treated it a little too much as a gift that was ours to use as we pleased rather than an investment made for a greater return to the kingdom. He felt every bit as strongly about his investment in our ministry as the Master who distributed talents to His servants (Matthew 25:14–30). Those who invested their talents for a tangible return were richly rewarded. The servant who fearfully and timidly hid the talent entrusted to him was deemed "a worthless servant."

Is this the singular perspective of a venture capitalist or the way most thoughtful givers approach giving in the kingdom? It might be more explicit in the realm of the marketplace, but experience shows that most giving, most of the time, is viewed by the giver as an investment in the kingdom through the work of a particular organization.

The woman who has taught school all her life and chooses to entrust a part of her assets to a ministry is essentially doing the same thing as the venture capitalist: investing for kingdom returns. Sometimes getters wonder why donors cease to be donors to their cause. Probably more often than we care to realize, it is because we considered the gift, once made, *our* money and left the giver out of the equation. What could be more counter to the true spirit of giving in the kingdom? The lessons of gifts as investments are many:

Ideas animate gifts.

Poorly informed gatherers lead with *needs*. Investors respond to *ideas*. What can leverage the resources I have to give into growing the kingdom values that God has put in my heart? Dollars chase ideas and never catch up with needs.

Planning and competence encourage confidence.

Parting with hard-earned resources is never an easy decision, even for the most spiritually sensitive giver. If the organization can demonstrate a thoughtful plan and the leadership ability to carry out the idea that needs funding, the investor can be more confident and generous. If it cannot, would anyone argue that they deserve the gift?

Skin in the game.

I've thought about that phrase many times since hearing it in relation to a proposed gift, and it makes all the sense in the world. If the organization comes to a prospective giver and says, "Here's an idea we have. If you take all the risks, we'll give it a try," what kind of confidence does that instill? But if the organization can say, "Here are the resources we are committing to bring to the table (it might be other financial resources, it might be dedicated time of existing staff)," it conveys a partnership in a promising venture rather than a shot in the dark.

The investor has a right to expect execution and regular reporting.
The reason the giver is interested in giving *through* (not to) your organization in the first place is that your track record and current leadership demonstrate the potential for a good return for the kingdom. If indeed the organization has entered into a partnership with the giver, it should make every effort to be transparent about the progress of the venture, both along the way and at the completion of the project.

Then there is evaluation.
The investor I talked with wasn't demanding success. He wanted every "talent" invested well. If the idea failed, even with thoughtful execution, he didn't see the investment as a failure at all. Outcomes are never irrelevant, but they are not the only goal of an investment. Even so, success or failure calls for clear evaluation. What was done well? What was ill conceived? What were the unanticipated challenges and how did we adapt? Objective evaluation is a level of accountability that is a reasonable expectation of the donor/investor, and will be the catalyst for future investment.

RELATIONSHIPS COUNT
What elevates detached, transactional giving into meaningful, joyful giving is relationship. Dropping coins in the lap of a street beggar may be satisfying and entirely "right" for that situation, but that "transaction" pales in comparison to an interactive relationship between the object of giving and the giver. Or the relationship between the ministry and a supporter of that ministry. Or, as most often happens, the relationship between the representative of the organization (getter) and the giver.

An occupational hazard of the gatherer is to think their part in the giving transaction is more important than it often is. The person engaged in calling men and women to give in the kingdom should not think of themselves more highly than they ought. The more enduring relationship is the donor's with the organization and his or her calling before God as a steward in the kingdom. Here are some things to keep in mind to maintain these relationships well.

You can have too many relationships.

Personalities differ greatly, both in givers and getters. Energy levels, spiritual maturity, responsibilities of vocation and family life, geographical location, personality, and interest can and do affect the quality and depth of relationship. An occupational hazard for the getter is attempting too many giving relationships. Many people with responsibility for major gifts to their organization have lists a mile long in terms of number and an inch deep in terms of significance. While on paper it appears there is great coverage and productivity, a sober evaluation usually exposes way too many obligations to truly serve the individuals in your care. That, of course, begs the question, "How many donor relationships can/should one productive major gifts officer have? Five hundred? Three hundred? Two hundred?"

Of course it depends on many factors. In my experience, we used to talk about "managing" two hundred relationships. We have found that is probably impossible. We've shrunk our "200" lists to "150" and it is still high. Here's a way to think about attempting to manage 150 relationships. To be a good steward on behalf of your organization and a good friend to those who support you, think in these ratios: there should be twenty-five to fifty individuals with whom you are proactive and whom you believe have interest and ability to support your work. Your primary responsibility to them is to discover their level of interest, capacity, and the animating passions of their support for kingdom enterprises. There should also be twenty-five to seventy-five individuals who have demonstrated through their giving and statements of support that they already care deeply about the work your organization does. This is the group of men and women who require your regular interaction. They need to be introduced to

GIVING AND GETTING IN THE KINGDOM

ways to be involved in the life of the organization. These interactions should build to key moments in their relationship with the organization when they are challenged to bring their resources to bear in their area of passion and your area of opportunity. Another general group of individuals may comprise twenty-five or so individuals who, by reason of circumstance, have given all they can to your organization. While they offer little or no capacity for further giving, they deserve the love and care of the organization for their past giving and their continued care for your kingdom work. In fact, how we treat those who no longer have capacity to support us financially is a good test of our commitment to kingdom values.

Does that sound like enough relationships for one person to engage in? I think so! Establishing, maintaining, and growing relationships is the most difficult and rewarding work of getting in the kingdom. It is both the right thing to do and the most important thing to do. Thoughtful Christian stewards rarely demand this kind of attention, but they deserve it. Determine a manageable number of relationships and get to work!

How you respond makes a difference.

Every current, past, and potential supporter of your organization is worthy of being appropriately served by your organization. It is inconsequential whether they have high capacity to give or not. A good way to guard your heart and priorities in this case is to resist looking up the giving record before you answer a question or research a complaint. People will often call, write, or register a question or concern via another person when they perceive something that could affect their relationship with the organization. That is why it is unconscionable to ignore an inquiry. Our response should be prompt, thorough, and in a spirit worthy of the kingdom. Criticism or challenge is one of the greatest gifts a giver can give to you and the organization. Buried in even the harshest criticism is often a grain of insight that can make you better as an organization and as a person. "A rebuke impresses a [person] of discernment more than a hundred lashes a fool" (Proverbs 17:10).

> ESTABLISHING, MAINTAINING, AND GROWING RELATIONSHIPS IS THE MOST DIFFICULT AND REWARDING WORK OF GETTING IN THE KINGDOM.

How you initiate makes a difference.

Being responsive is one level of care for relationships. Initiating and growing a meaningful relationship between an individual and your organization is what differentiates average programs from the very best ones. No one would deny that relationships are a lot of work! Maintaining healthy, growing relationships with family, spouses, close friends, and co-workers can require plenty of time and consume plenty of energy. But being proactive with individuals who harbor love and care for the work of your organization is what thoughtful gatherers in the kingdom do—and do well. We will say much more about this in chapter 6, but few if any relationships grow without intentionality. This could not be more true than for the relationship of the giver to your work.

Listen. Give. Love.

True givers have a lot of wisdom, not just about giving but about life. People who have figured out the important matter of resources within the kingdom have figured out quite a few other fundamental truths as well. So to build relationships on behalf of your cause, do a lot of listening. You will grow as a person, but you will also learn what the giver cares deeply about. That can inform who you introduce them to in your organization and will lead you to areas of giving that will be as satisfying to them as beneficial to you.

And give. Give your time and attention. Give meaningful information and feedback. Give thoughtful (not expensive) gifts that demonstrate that you care for them as individuals. Give prompt and thorough replies to questions, even if it is time-consuming to research the answers. Giving can and should be a two-way exchange. It is a key component of a loving relationship.

And finally, love the giver. All meaningful relationships have the qualities of concern, care, hospitality, and fondness. In the relationship of the donor to the organization, the appropriate object of that kind of care and fondness is the organization and its people, not principally the getter. The gatherer who allows himself to become the primary object of the giver's affection is not serving the organization well. Remember, the getter is merely the link between the donor and the organization.

> **TRUE GIVERS GRAVITATE TO BIG IDEAS THAT CAN RESULT IN GAINS FOR THE ORGANIZATION AND THE KINGDOM.**

But love, extended well, will enable the giver to interact in meaningful and satisfying ways with the organization. That is a win for the organization, growth for the giver, and a properly diminished place for the getter.

BIG IDEAS ATTRACT BIG GIFTS

We have said it in many ways. True givers possess uncommon wisdom and insight. They give freely, but not lightly. Investing in the kingdom is serious business with eternal consequences. Why, then, do organizations persist in presenting small ideas? It could be because of lack of vision and energy. Granted, it is easier to ask a giver to help balance the organization's budget than to conceive a project that will move the organization forward in a dramatic way—and has the potential to fail! But true givers gravitate to big ideas that can result in gains for the organization and the kingdom. If the leadership of the organization has given up on big ideas and settled for a defensive approach that will simply maintain the status quo, they usually receive the level of support they deserve.

Of course, balancing a budget can be a big idea if the budget is carefully constructed and made reasonably transparent to the giver.

If all the physical and human resources of the organization are marshaled for a clear mission and purpose, balancing the budget *is* a big idea. But constructing and presenting that kind of budget takes just the vision and energy we are talking about. And, of course, a big, jazzy idea can lack planning and integrity. A plan for a major ministry expansion that has only tangential relationship to the mission of the organization and dubious prospects for sustainability is not a big idea, it's a bad idea! So, what are the hallmarks of ideas that can attract big gifts? Consider this observation from a gifted giver. He is the CEO of a Fortune 500 company. He listens to big ideas within his company almost every day: how to expand the business into a promising market, how to dramatically reduce operating cost to improve profit margin. But he also talks often with representatives from the nonprofit sector: relief organizations, hospitals, microfinance lenders, colleges and universities. When I asked him what is a common mistake that these representatives make when talking to him, his answer was quick and sure: "Please don't come to me with an 'order list' already thought out, where my only decision is how much to give!" When the organization has done all the thinking and only wants capital from the giver, they have forfeited not only wise counsel but also a deeper relationship and, most probably, the big gift as well.

Big ideas are mission-centered. Their implementation will move the organization forward in the unique work it is called to do. Big ideas are carefully conceived. They are not presented for funding until the impact on the organization, sustainability of the project beyond implementation, and initial cost projections are considered. And big ideas are subject to change—not in a "whatever the giver wants" sort of way but in a "what is the best way to accomplish our goal" way.

Many givers take joy in sustaining a cause they love. They deserve an organization's careful planning and accountability. But many more reserve their largest gifts for the organization that demonstrates vision, creativity, and flexibility in boldly pursuing their God-given mission. They are eager to invest not in a sure thing but in a big idea with the potential to leverage their gifts for the sake of the kingdom.

THE BEST GIVERS RARELY LOOK WEALTHY

She lives in my town in one of the more modest homes in our community. My house is bigger and more expensively furnished. Until a few years ago, she mowed her own lawn. Her car, like her home, is older and unassuming. The organization I serve knows her well, but no one else would even suspect she was a donor, let alone one of the largest donors to our cause.

Anomaly? Not in the least. As I think about the largest donors I have interacted with over the years, they fall in two categories. They either resemble the person I just described: quiet, unassuming, and with a very modest standard of living. This profile was made rather famous by the book, *The Millionaire Next Door,* by Thomas J. Stanley and William D. Danko.[13] When the authors went about profiling the "wealthy" in America, they began by looking at those with expensive homes and cars. What they discovered was that relatively few of these individuals were truly wealthy—they were simply spending higher incomes than most other Americans. The research found, instead, that many people of true wealth live well below their means in housing, automobiles, and lifestyle.

The second common profile of potential larger givers is people who, by their occupation, are known to have significant income and wealth. But even in this more conspicuous group, most clearly live well below their means as a matter of conviction. The best givers rarely look wealthy.

One of the occupational hazards of being a fundraiser is the inevitable association with wealth. If we don't guard our hearts (see chapter 6), envy, ingratiation, and, perhaps deadliest of all, imitation can creep in and compromise our effective service in Christ's kingdom. But the discerning getter can see beyond—no—*below* the visible wealth to the heart of the giver.

With few exceptions, those who *appear* wealthy—conspicuous consumption, manner, and bearing—are often not the gifted givers we seek. In fact, that very appearance *may* be a sign of spiritual immaturity in the matter of giving. (Though we must be cautious here: only God knows a person's heart.) When it comes to wealth and propensity to give, appearances can lead us badly astray. That is why genuine engagement and conversation with all who show interest in your cause is a far better gauge of significant potential and willingness to give than any external evidence. That discipline will also help guard the getter from shallow judgments about who is and who is not a person of wealth.

> THOSE WHO *APPEAR* WEALTHY ARE OFTEN NOT THE GIFTED GIVERS WE SEEK.

Look at your own group of current donors. For the most part, those who give best probably don't match our skewed judgments about wealth. Probably those who *will* give to us in the future will be those who either clearly live well below their means or show little if any evidence of wealth. By and large, the best donors rarely look wealthy.

The mind of the giver matters. Listening attentively and adapting every approach to the individual demonstrates that we value the giver more than the gift.

CHAPTER

HOW **MONEY FLOWS**

Money is better than poverty, if only for financial reasons.
—Woody Allen

The rich and poor have this in common:
The LORD is the Maker of them all.
—Proverbs 22:2

A LOT FROM A FEW MAKES ALL THE DIFFERENCE

You are in a planning meeting with a group of businessmen and women to have an initial conversation about a project to raise $100,000 within the next year. Your organization has three hundred active donors. Almost invariably someone will speak up and say something like, "I don't see what the big problem is. With three hundred donors, surely we can get one hundred gifts of $1,000 and be done with it!"

This is a common misconception in the sphere of giving and getting. It is critically important that giver and getter alike be aware how wealth is distributed and how it is given in the nonprofit sector. How money actually flows has a huge impact on the strategy we employ to accumulate needed resources. It also helps the thoughtful Christian steward rise to their responsibility to adequately fund the project they are called to invest in.

The Federal Reserve Board *Survey of Consumer Finances* reveals that 1 percent of the population of the United States holds 34.3 percent of the wealth. Ten percent of Americans possess 71 percent of the wealth. In contrast, 40 percent of the population holds 0.2 percent of the aggregate wealth in the United States. While our constituencies do not necessarily mirror these statistics, they surely resemble them. And we ignore this reality at our own peril.

In chapter 12, we will see how this reality is fleshed out in planning for any fundraising project. But here it is important to note that wealth is not distributed evenly, neither does it come in evenly to any organization. The old and fairly reliable 80/20 rule (80 percent of your gift income will come from 20 percent of your donors) has been replaced in many organizations by the 95/5 rule. Whether this is healthy is another question. But the wise organization will take time to consider how wealth is distributed in any group of potential givers (whether 10 or 100,000). They will also consider what level of gifts will be required to achieve their desired financial outcome.

An example from a large organization.

A Christian nonprofit organization recently completed a successful five-year, $250 million campaign. They have a large, national constituency. In fact, in the course of the five years, over 28,000 households contributed to the total. But let's take a closer look at the numbers. In reality, about 1 percent (313 to be exact) of the contributors gave a whopping $194.3 million (77 percent) of the total. Some will say, "But, that is a large organization and a large campaign. Surely the numbers are different for the smaller organization with a smaller goal." In truth, small campaigns mirror the same ratios.

An example from a smaller organization.

In a recent year, a smaller organization had total gift income of $273,095 from 328 donors. The largest gift was $80,000 (29 percent of total gift income from one donor!). The top ten gifts totaled $131,500 (48 percent of total gift income from 3 percent of the donors). The top hundred gifts (30 percent of individual donors) gave 76 percent of total gift income! The remaining 24 percent came from all the rest. Whether a smaller goal or a larger one, almost invariably a lot from a few makes all the difference.

The lesson from how money flows to individuals and to organizations as gifts is that this reality must infuse stewardship planning, by organizations and donors alike. The playing field is not flat. Not only is *desire* to be involved as a donor a factor, the *capacity* of your constituency must be factored in as well. Of course, *every* gift is important, and we have already seen that generosity is not best measured by the amount of the gift. Nonetheless, planning for the kind of gifts your church or organization will achieve must take into account how wealth is distributed in any grouping of potential givers and what level of gifts will be required to achieve the desired financial outcome.

For any organization contemplating funding its mission, either operational support or special project, there are several critical questions to ask yourself:

Do you have a relative handful (five to fifty) of prospective givers with the financial capacity and level of engagement to provide 25 to 60 percent of the total gift income needed? If not, your goal is probably unrealistic.

If you have determined you have a small number of individuals with the capacity and willingness to lead your effort with substantial giving, are you willing to challenge this group of men and women *first* as you embark on your financial goal? This is important if you really agree that a few gifts will make all the difference in any fundraising effort. If your most capable group is unwilling or unable to provide a significant portion of your total (25 to 60 percent), chances are you will never reach your total with gifts from all the rest of your willing constituents. While that may sound harsh or faithless, it is a proven reality in hundreds of settings both in the secular and the kingdom realms. We make the point in chapter 12 that God, of course, can provide resources for His work in any way He chooses; but the wise organization takes heed of how God typically provides.

The organization has its own stewardship role in educating its thoughtful stewards on how money is distributed and how it tends to come in. Part of leading the thoughtful giver is to demonstrate how money flows and what gifts are typically needed for the success of the effort. If capable givers understand the realities of gifts needed to fund any project, they most often rise to the challenge.

For any giver contemplating funding the mission of an organization, either operational support or special project:

Explore with the organization how the leadership anticipates gifts coming in. In their best estimation, what level of gifts will they need to succeed? Have they thought through the possibilities well?

Consider, to the best of your ability, how your individual stewardship toward their project will be instrumental to their achieving their goal. Apart from your personal stewardship obligations, can (should?) your gift be a strategic component in achieving the goals of the organization and in raising the sights of other potential donor/investors?

In this world, a lot from a few makes all the difference. In God's kingdom, however, *every* gift is important, and there are numerous reasons why.

WHY LITTLE GIFTS COUNT BIG

Without question, a few larger gifts make a huge difference—often the deciding difference—in any fundraising effort. But *every* gift is important. We dare not value the large gift sent by a broker on behalf of the client over the crinkled five-dollar bill stuffed in an envelope.

Here is why. First of all, in God's kingdom the heart of the giver is infinitely more important than the financial capacity of the giver. Jesus' observation of the poor widow confirms it. "Jesus . . . watched the crowd putting their money into the temple treasure. Many rich people threw in large amounts. But a poor widow came and put in two very small copper coins worth only a fraction of a penny. . . . Jesus said, 'I tell you the truth, this poor widow has put more into the treasury than all the others. They all gave out of their wealth, but she, out of her poverty, put in everything—all she had to live on'" (Mark 12:41–44). Far from a quaint story, Jesus took time to convey a profound, eternal truth to His disciples. Giving "all she had to live on" was precious in God's sight. We who gather gifts for the kingdom dare not take a lesser view of the small gift given with great sacrifice than our Lord Himself. That is reason in itself to celebrate, remember, and treasure the small gift and its giver.

> WE DARE NOT VALUE THE LARGE GIFT SENT BY A BROKER ON BEHALF OF THE CLIENT OVER THE CRINKLED FIVE-DOLLAR BILL STUFFED IN AN ENVELOPE.

But there are several other reasons we must not despise the small gift. First, small gifts often "grow up" to be larger gifts. Very few give the largest gift they are capable of early in the relationship with an organization. How we value, steward, and thank for the small gift often determines our worthiness for a larger commitment.

It was my first month on the new job. Quite apart from any of my influence, we received a gift of $1 million! As the excitement rippled through our department, I looked up this couple's previous giving. I expected to see a long history of giving building up to this momentous gift. Instead, what I found was one previous gift—about ten years earlier—for $100! It was in response to a phon-a-thon call. Who knows but without that prior gift and my institution's response to that gift, the larger gift might never have come to pass. Don't despise the small gift. In God's economy, it might already be a very large one! Or, it might "grow," through patience and relationship, into a transformational gift.

There is one more reason to treasure the small gift. As we have seen, in almost any giving effort, a preponderance of all the gifts will be small gifts. The number of individuals will be disproportionately large compared to the dollar total of those gifts. But what do those gifts represent? Certainly they represent thoughtful, perhaps even sacrificial, stewardship decisions just like the larger gifts. These gifts almost surely come with prayers and goodwill toward the kingdom work of your organization. We may never know the value of those gifts and prayers to the success of our kingdom work. Indeed, at the last day, we may find that they were the difference between mediocrity and significance. We dismiss or undervalue the "small" gift at our own peril. Little gifts surely count big.

TOWARD IDEAS, AWAY FROM NEEDS

Money flows unevenly because wealth is distributed unevenly. But there is another factor that influences the flow of money—ideas. It has been well said that money chases ideas but never catches up with need. Why, then, do so many organizations resort to appeals to *need* rather than share *ideas* that will resonate with thoughtful Christian stewards? Here we return to the important topic of putting away the tin cup. Way too many organizations, formed to advance the kingdom, have cooled in their passion and creativity, and are consumed with maintenance, cash flow, and balanced budgets. Somehow the passion for relevance has devolved into passive acceptance of incremental growth, or even mere subsistence of their mission and influence. They have become like our thinking about street beggars holding a tin cup. "No plan for the money beyond subsistence. Any amount will do. We don't need to relate, just give, please!" No wonder money does not readily flow to those organizations. Ideas, rooted in careful planning, will accelerate the flow of money to your organization.

TO PEOPLE OVER PROGRAMS
In the work of gathering resources for kingdom work, we have heard it many times: "We don't give to bricks and mortar. We reserve our giving for people." Actually, that sentiment is understandable in the context of the kingdom. If the kingdom of God is eternal and the "things" of this world, including buildings and their furnishings, are not, why would someone invest in the temporal? The answer is, if the school building in Kenya will enable teachers and students to connect in beneficial ways for the students and their future families and communities, then, of course it is good stewardship to invest in a building that is temporal. There are many temporal "tools" that can be used for eternal purposes.

The lesson is to always differentiate between the means and the ends of any project. The comment "I don't give to bricks and mortar" contains the stark truth that things are temporal, people are not. But if things are useful tools to accomplish the eternal, every thoughtful steward gets that. Things—buildings, cars, communication networks—can and should be instruments to greater ends, such as meeting immediate human needs and attending to the destiny of their souls. That requires the temporal to be utilitarian. For example, an economy rather than a luxury car should do to transport the people you serve. The importance of people over the tools of serving people must shine through all of our appeals to the giver. They have a kingdom perspective. We must maintain one as well.

TO RESULTS OVER INSTITUTIONS
The day is quickly passing when any organization—church, denomination, social agency—is worthy of support because, well, because

of the very fact that it exists and has a history of performance. The Builder generation is more content to support an "institution" than their Boomer offspring, let alone the Gen Ys! There is far more urgency for today's nonprofit to demonstrate relevance and performance, regardless of history or reputation. Money flows more readily to demonstrable results than to longevity, reputation, or name.

> BE THE KIND OF ORGANIZATION THAT IS DELIVERING ON ITS PROMISE TO THE PUBLIC, AND BY GOD'S GRACE, MONEY WILL FLOW IN YOUR DIRECTION.

And, frankly, that is good and healthy for the nonprofit sector. There are over one million nonprofit entities in the United States alone, each one established to meet a particular need. That is laudable. But the founding sentiment is far less important today than its current relevance and performance. Determining current effectiveness calls for more reflection and transparency and less presumption of current support based on past performance. The growing reality of the flow of money is away from tradition and toward demonstrable results. Be the kind of organization that is delivering on its promise to the public, and by God's grace, money will flow in your direction.

PART II

GETTING:
A WAY OF BEING

Much more of our success in financial work depends
on what we are and what we do when we are not soliciting
financial help, than what we say or do at the time we
make our financial appeals. It is of transcendent importance
that we be pure in heart, unselfish in spirit, and
unswervingly and courageously loyal to our Lord Jesus Christ.

—**JOHN R. MOTT,** long-serving leader of the YMCA

CHAPTER

6

THE

MESSENGER MATTERS

*And Caspian knelt and kissed the Lion's paw. "Welcome, Prince,"
said Aslan. "Do you feel yourself sufficient to take up the
Kingship of Narnia?" "I—I don't think I do, Sir," said Caspian.
"I'm only a kid." "Good," said Aslan. "If you had felt yourself
sufficient, it would have been a proof that you were not."*
—C. S. Lewis, *The Chronicles of Narnia: The Lion, the Witch and the Wardrobe*

GUARD YOUR HEART

The wisdom of Proverbs is unassailable: "Above all else, guard your heart, for it is the wellspring of life" (4:23). It is a privilege to ask God's people for God's resources, for His work. The rewards are many, but so are the pitfalls. If we remind ourselves of the rewards and guard our hearts against the pitfalls, there will be joy in the task and confidence we are faithfully serving in the kingdom. Or to put it in Robert Payton's terms, we can be sure we are living *for* philanthropy, not *off* philanthropy.

If you have been engaged in this work for years, you have experienced the rich rewards of your vocation. If you are just starting out, there are several things you can look forward to.

1. True givers have a lot figured out about what is important in life.

It is a common question from a seatmate on the plane or a first meeting at a social engagement: "So, what do you do?" My short answer is, "I raise support for my organization." The reply is usually something like, "Oh, you're a fundraiser. I could never do that." Of course, what they usually mean is that asking for money from anyone would be one of the last things they would care to do. It would be awkward and uncomfortable to be engaged in asking someone to part with their wealth. But I am able to tell them that I have the privilege of meeting remarkable people. They are not remarkable because they are achievers or are wealthy, though many of them are. They are remarkable because true givers have learned a lot about what is important in life.

True givers are well past a primary concern about their own well-being. They are decidedly other-centered. They tend to see the big picture of the condition of this world and have an intimate knowledge of the One who created it. They realize the utter truth that this life is a vapor—a mere dot on the continuum of eternity. Seeing life from God's point of view provides a peace and outlook that is winsome and solid and true. Yes, these are the kinds of people whom gatherers in the kingdom have the privilege of knowing. How many vocations provide the opportunity to regularly observe and interact with whole and effective people? They model (imperfectly, of course) what it means to be a faithful disciple of Christ in a complicated and broken world.

2. You have opportunity for an incredible variety of experiences.

The list of opportunities is a long one. In the service of many national and international organizations, there is travel, which will broaden your understanding of the world (and test your patience!). You will come to know a wide variety of people who will stretch you intellectually and spiritually and sharpen your abilities to interact with a wide variety of people. Because gathering in the kingdom is so important (money fuels vision), you will be at the table formulating the goals and strategies of your organization. This is both personally satisfying and an affirmation of your calling.

3. You grow in your ability to influence people.
There is no getting around it. Gathering in the kingdom requires the gift of genuinely engaging people and calling them to faithful, generous stewardship. Influencing people and the course of events of your organization is not to be taken lightly. It has the ability to change and grow you, those you interact with, and the organization you serve.

4. Most important, you get to spend every working hour in direct service of Christ's kingdom.
It was toward the end of my seminary training. Tony Campolo was addressing the roomful of men and women who would most likely spend their vocational lives in direct service to the kingdom as pastors, leaders in parachurch ministries, or social service agencies. He was painting a rather grim picture of the state of things and the many obstacles to success in our chosen vocations. Then he said something that has stayed close to me my whole life. While I can't re-create his inimitable style, I can convey the import of what he said: "Do you realize that you are the most privileged people in the world? Why? Of the billions of people on the planet who are farmers and traders and janitors and factory workers, you get to spend your whole working day and life in direct service to Christ's kingdom." It is one of the highest and most overlooked privileges of getting in the kingdom.

These are some of the rich rewards of being called to get in the kingdom. But there are pitfalls that need to be anticipated. Of course every vocation has its own set of occupational hazards. What are the hazards of getting in the kingdom?

1. Taking credit away from the thoughtful Christian steward.

It is easy in the course of a campaign or a career to shift credit for the success of the effort from the givers to the organization or, more insidiously, to the fundraiser. If success comes in getting, people (board members, CEOs, staff, other observers) will often congratulate you on your success. This is gracious, of course. And it does reflect the reality that if no one conceives a project, puts things in place to make the project known, and "sells" the project to the donor/investor, success seldom comes. But the wise quickly turn around the credit to the thoughtful stewards who have come forward to make the success possible—not in a cloying, ingratiating way but in honest reflection of the integral place of engaged and generous friends in the sustenance of the organization.

2. Stealing credit from God Himself.

If indeed God is the "giver of all good gifts," and if He is truly at work in the organization and those who support it, doesn't it make sense that, ultimately, credit must be given to Him? In my experience, donors and organizations alike are good about honoring God with the results of any particular gift or series of gifts that enable the advance of the mission of the organization. But the careless fundraiser can come to assume that their part in the giving equation is central. It is wise to heed the counsel of Proverbs: "All a man's ways seem innocent to him, but motives are weighed by the Lord" (16:2). Appropriately giving and taking credit is part of the grace incumbent on the gatherer in Christ's kingdom. It puts the role of the giver and the getter in balance with God's work in His domain.

3. Envy.

Envy is a deadly sin not reserved for any particular person or vocation. But, it can become a stumbling block to effective service for gatherers in the kingdom. The reasons are obvious. Many involved in gathering resources for kingdom work spend a preponderance of time with men and women of wealth. While many of them live well below their means, many still live at a level that is conspicuously different than the average person. This can mean spending significant time at nice homes or country clubs or thriving businesses. (We will leave the discussion of the proportions of these experiences compared to the tedious grunt work of our profession for another section.) Nonetheless, a sense of entitlement and envy can creep into the mind-set of gatherers. *If I am called to serve those who have significant wealth, surely it is my right to enjoy some of the benefits of that wealth.* Such envy and assumption of equivalence can be deadly.

There is another aspect of getting where envy can creep in. It can be found in the success of other kingdom enterprises. "Why did *they* receive that multimillion dollar gift? Why not me? Why not us?" Again the words of Proverbs are true: "A heart at peace gives life to the body, but envy rots the bones" (14:30). As in every aspect of our moral housekeeping, we must remind ourselves of what is good and right and true, and flee temptations that would distract us from our calling in Christ.

4. Spiritual torpor.

Torpor is a wonderfully descriptive, if not common, word. It means "sluggish inactivity or inertia." Spiritual torpor is particularly insidious for any involved in an organization whose very existence and mission is related to service in the kingdom, because we can (mostly unconsciously) rationalize that every activity we engage in is a service to God. It is that very service that can crowd out our daily accountability to the God we serve and to others who can help keep our souls aligned with the eternal. The enemies of personal piety are the usual suspects: Extreme busyness. Lack of care for our bodies. Letting ourselves slip into the ungodly mind-set that what we do and what we think is no one's business but ours, especially if it is not hurtful to anyone else. Letting the exigencies of the moment—finishing up a campaign, making one more call, etc.—crowd out our ultimate purpose for living and being as citizens of His eternal kingdom. There are many resources, human and divine, to keep us on a purposeful path, but the first step is to understand the depths of our frailty and wandering affections. The writer of Hebrews said it well: "But encourage one another daily, as long as it is called Today, so that none of you may be hardened by sin's deceitfulness" (Hebrews 3:13). Put yourself in places and with people who can frequently rescue you from your sinful self and keep you fruitful in His kingdom. Above all else, guard your heart, for it is the wellspring of life (Proverbs 4:23).

LOVE YOUR CAUSE

Seeking funds for any Christian enterprise is hard work. It can be life-giving to labor in a field for which God has given you a passion. It can also be excruciating to engage in the task without passion for the mission. Fortunately, it is usually passion for the mission that first draws people to any organization. It might be your alma mater, which shaped your life. Or possibly a youth ministry that transformed the life of one of your children. Or a relief organization that matches your passion to lift the poor.

The wise gatherer knows that fundraising skills may be transferable, but heart and passion are not. As much as it lies within your control, follow your God-given passion for service to the kind of organization that has the potential to fulfill that passion. It will make you a better pastor, a better board member, a better ministry leader, a better development officer. Serving in your area of passion will also bring you more joy, and will probably make you more fruitful in your service. Of course, you can allow the mission of the organization to win your heart. The biblical principle of "Where your treasure is, there will your heart be also" applies to vocation as well.

If your treasure (vocational energy) is fully invested, it is likely, if not inevitable, that your heart will follow. Part of being the messenger God wants you to be is to fall in love and stay in love with the mission of your organization. If that should falter, it might be time to give way to someone else who can wholeheartedly take up the task. Service in Christ's kingdom requires nothing less than your best.

GIVE BEFORE YOU ASK

It was my first day on the job. Directing the development effort of a ministry I loved was a dream come true. What a responsibility I had been given, and such an opportunity to influence the future of my organization! I couldn't wait to get started. I needed to get to know my team. I needed to lay out meaningful goals that would stretch us. I needed to get out and meet the champions of our organization— and those who could be. But it occurred to me on day one that I could not set a vision for gathering financial resources without first committing my own resources to the effort. That very day I made a long-term commitment to regularly give to the organization I serve. No one but our gift receipting personnel knew it. And, of course, my commitment did not tip the balance sheet of my organization! But in ways I have discovered over the years, giving *first* enabled more joyful, effective service.

> DO NOT NEGLECT TO GIVE BEFORE YOU ASK.

Do not neglect to give before you ask. In fact, I believe it is unconscionable for a person to challenge another person to give to an organization that he has neglected to make an important part of his own stewardship. Who would know? God, of course, who sees all, would view this lack of integrity. Do you know who else would know? You would—and so would many thoughtful Christian stewards you would call on. Your reticence—your lack of sincerity—would affect your ability to advocate and your passion to ask. The true giver has a sense of whether or not they are talking with a kindred spirit. Give before you ask. The God who sees your sincere heart will reward your faithful, quiet stewardship.

BE A COMPLETE PROFESSIONAL

I've been asked a hundred times, "What qualities do you look for in a fundraising professional?" My list seems predictable to me, but since I am asked often, I will share it for whatever benefit it may be.

The nonnegotiables:

1. A childlike faith in Christ.

How do children approach anything they are serious about? With abandon. With persistence. With the joy of discovery. It doesn't take long to discern if faith is integral to the life and work of the applicant or merely a cultural identity. Passion to know and serve Christ is a necessary prerequisite for service in the kingdom.

2. Evidence of crystal integrity.

While sometimes it is possible to discern integrity (or lack thereof) in the course of a conversation, the truer test is what others have observed about the integrity of your life. References count big here. There are many possible "tells" of insincerity or even lack of integrity: exaggerations on resumes, hesitant comments by references, or inconsistencies in the narrative of their life.

3. Personal experience in generous giving.

One could easily slip into the world's mentality on personal finances: "my giving and my finances are nobody's business but mine." However, what could be more telling about someone's capacity to elicit generous giving from others than their own experience? Ask them about a joyful giving experience of their own. How important is personal giving to them? Have they ever taught others what it means to be rich toward God? It is a delicate area for sure, but if they cannot articulate what it means to be a thoughtful steward of resources, how can you expect them to call others to it?

4. An understanding of and passion for the mission.
Passion for the mission may come with doing the work of your organization, but understanding the mission can be gained well before the interview. Has the applicant taken the time to understand your mission and how it differentiates you from similar organizations? If they have not, they are either careless about your interview or, worse yet, more interested in a job than in carrying forward the mission of your organization. Look and listen for evidence of passion for your mission.

Qualities to look for:

1. Care about appearance.
One way to honor those we serve (givers in the kingdom) is to groom and dress in a way that is never inappropriate. Expensive clothing is never necessary, but modest and professional dress is. Rule of thumb? I've never felt overdressed for an appointment or social function with givers, but I have felt underdressed on several occasions. Lean toward overdressed. It demonstrates respect for the individual and for the organization you serve.

2. Ability to engage in meaningful conversation.
True givers come in all ages and many different personalities and interests. It does not take very long into a conversation to discern if a person is interesting in their own right, and more important, genuinely interested in other people. Don't just listen to questions they answer, listen to questions they ask. Both are essential for meaningful relationships to flourish. Do they appear to be one-dimensional in their interests, or do you discern a curiosity about life in general and people in particular?

3. Demonstrated care for others.

While references can help illuminate a caring spirit, observations of your meeting with the applicant can be telling. Were they on time? How did they treat the receptionist? Did they ask and listen or merely sell themselves. Do their interests and involvements indicate care beyond themselves and their immediate family? You should be able to read these qualities—and you can be sure the givers in your organization will as well. Don't disappoint them.

4. Goal orientation.

While the essence of relating givers to the mission and work of your organization is building strong and lasting relationships, those relationships require discipline and intentionality on the part of the gatherer. The work of gathering (and it *is* work) requires the ability to envision outcomes and plan and execute the work to achieve those outcomes. All the relational skills in the world will fall short of the intentionality required to secure gifts of time, talent, and treasure from givers. Make sure the applicant possesses the will and ability and experience to set, achieve, and take joy in attaining meaningful, measurable goals.

> ALL THE RELATIONAL SKILLS IN THE WORLD WILL FALL SHORT OF THE INTENTIONALITY REQUIRED TO SECURE GIFTS OF TIME, TALENT, AND TREASURE FROM GIVERS.

5. A willingness to ask (see following section).

As you might have discerned by now, a willingness to call people to decision is a critical skill to possess. In fact, we deal with it in more depth in the following section.

6. The ability to listen.

For some reason, many think that the effective fundraiser is a good talker. You need someone who is well-spoken, quick to answer objections, and highly conversational. Experience teaches otherwise. It's not the good talker who excels at the fundraising task. It is the good listener. The adage, "God gave us two ears and one mouth so that we could listen and speak in those proportions," could not be more true than in the fundraising realm. Particularly when representing a cause, our inclination is to *tell*—what we are about, why a project is important, and why you should give. But without listening carefully and asking appropriate questions, we are often speaking *past* the thoughtful steward rather than *with* them. The true listener learns what animates a person's desire to give. The gifted listener hears when a potential donor has moved past objections or concerns and is ready to consider financial commitment. The patient listener knows when there is more work to be done before a commitment is possible. Listeners always outraise talkers.

> IT'S NOT THE GOOD TALKER WHO EXCELS AT THE FUNDRAISING TASK. IT IS THE GOOD LISTENER.

COMMIT TO THE ASK

I have interviewed scores of individuals for development roles in organizations I have served, as well as on the behalf of several clients. My questions are directed to draw out the attributes and qualities listed above. If I sense they line up well with the expectations of our development effort, I spend extra time on the expectation that they be willing to ask God's people for God's resources for God's work.

My first statement to the applicant on the subject of asking is something like, "Are you willing, at the appropriate time, to look a constituent in the eye and ask for a gift (sometimes a specific amount, sometimes not)? Before you answer, you should know that there is nothing wrong with you if your answer is no. But if you can't, or choose not to, please do not take this job—you will be miserable—and we will be miserable with you!"

Asking in the kingdom is not indiscriminate. In fact, it calls for a level of nuance and understanding that is a high standard for anyone engaged in getting for the kingdom. What are the guiding principles that are necessary to engage in the delicate matter of asking for financial commitment?

1. Relationship.

In asking for a financial gift, a meaningful relationship is nearly always essential. Two kinds of relationship are necessary. The first is a meaningful relationship between the organization and the potential donor. Wealth is an important qualification for any potential ask, but the relationship of the person to the organization is far more important. When did it begin? How? Whether a one-year or a forty-year relationship, what is the trajectory of that relationship? Highs? Lows? Plateaus? The answers can sometimes be painful but are always enlightening. A strong sense of the prevailing relationship of the donor to the organization can help determine whether or not to ask, when to ask, what project to ask for, and how much. Such an exercise is also a reminder that in nearly every case, love for the organization and its mission supersedes the messenger who is charged with deepening that relationship.

Those of us involved in gathering like to say, "People give to people, and I am the important one in the prospective donor's relationship with the organization." Taken to extremes, that way of thinking leads to territoriality ("I'm the only one who can advance this relationship") and a false sense of importance. But, of course, the messenger is important too. The messenger personifies the organization to the prospective giver (see "Nothing Never Happens" in chapter 7, p.103). Trust is a core component of any giving decision. If the messenger embodies the mission, culture, and identity of the organization, he is in a strong position to move the relationship forward. If he does not, he will act as a strong impediment to an atmosphere that encourages and enables generosity and support. So the messenger is a bridge between a relationship that (most often) predates his or her acquaintance with the donor and will exist long past the current messenger's tenure. That perspective will guard against shortsighted expediency and will foster a healthy relationship that will make the ask—and the gift—more likely.

2. *Common ground.*

Nothing can dampen the climate for a meaningful ask more than a transactional approach to getting the gift. It is too easy (and too common) to short-circuit a relational gift with the attempt at a transactional one. ("Here's our list of needs. Which one would you like to meet for us?") The gatherer is not an order taker or a collector! While no one would claim that as their role, it is all too easy to slip into the mode of the perfunctory visit and the obligatory ask ("We haven't seen a gift from you for over a year"). Genuine common ground with the potential giver takes time, creativity, and most of all, a caring, listening spirit. People can spot insincerity in an instant. Therefore, guarding your heart as a gatherer and intentionally listening for points of connection, both interpersonally and with the organization, will help provide a natural opportunity to call a giver to commitment.

> COMMON GROUND WITH THE POTENTIAL GIVER TAKES TIME, CREATIVITY, AND MOST OF ALL, A CARING, LISTENING SPIRIT.

3. *Permission to ask.*

We have already stated (as if it needed to be said) that asking for a gift is not an easy thing to do. Some are terrified at the prospect of talking with someone else about something that is considered, at least by the world's standards, private and nobody else's business. Others wrap the matter in the cloak of spirituality—"It is between them and God; I should not be interfering in that process." Many others simply never get around to it. They do not object in principle to asking for a gift to God's work, but for some reason, the prospective donor is never quite ready to be asked!

Here is a way to enable an ask: ask permission to ask. Here's what I mean. You've taken the time to understand the person's relationship with the organization. You have patiently established common ground. You have carefully and winsomely shared the project at hand and how it relates to the mission and future of the organization. Instead of plowing ahead with a specific request for a gift, do the unexpected. Restate your conversation to date. Reiterate the important points, both of your comments and theirs. Then ask the prospective donor if they would be willing to receive a specific proposal from you at a near point in the future. If you've laid the groundwork appropriately, how many people would respond by saying, "No, I am unwilling to receive or react to a specific proposal"? In my experience, almost no one. If they say yes to a willingness to receive a proposal, they have essentially told you that this is an area of interest to them and that a gift of some kind is a real possibility. Moreover, they are willing to have another conversation about a possible gift! That makes the initial gift conversation much more comfortable for the getter and the giver. It provides opportunity for the gatherer to rethink all that has been communicated and put it into a cogent proposal that will make sense to the giver and honor the fact that you have listened to them. Finally, it makes the call for the follow-up meeting a whole lot easier. Before you ask, ask permission to ask.

4. Ask.

Your conversation about a possible gift has progressed well. You have given plenty of opportunity for feedback and believe there is a genuine interest in the proposed program. You have asked for permission to ask and it has been granted. You have carefully put together a proposal. It is thoughtful, clear, and as brief as possible, incorporating only the elements that are clearly important to the prospective donor. Even though you will present it orally and in person, it is written in such a way that you would be pleased to leave it with the person as a summary of your conversation.

Now the moment is upon you. It is time to call for the question. There may be nothing more intimate or telling in your relationship than this question, eye to eye and face-to-face: "Would you consider a gift of $_____ for (<u>purpose</u>) , over _____ period of time?" You have asked the question. Now instead of talking over yourself or the giver who is considering your ask, just quietly listen and wait. You have fulfilled your responsibility as a gatherer; let them do their job as a thoughtful Christian steward. Their verbal and nonverbal reaction will tell you almost everything.

5. Listen.

Listen with your eyes and your ears. What are they "saying"? If you have communicated and listened well in your interactions on this project, you may well hear the sweet words, "I think we can do that." But often, because communication is fallible, you may hear, "not now," "not this project," or "not this amount." This is not a sign of failure. It means your proposal is being thoughtfully considered. But you cannot appropriately respond until you have appropriately listened.

6. Respond.

The greatest respect you can show a thoughtful steward is to patiently, thoroughly address any and all questions and concerns he or she raises. Some may be detail questions you can answer on the spot ("Sure, you can fulfill this commitment over five years instead of three. Our board has already made provision for that."). Other concerns may require more time and counsel to address ("We were looking to endow this program with your gift, but if you want this gift to be totally expended over the next ten years, I will need to confer with our CEO and the board to make sure this is workable."). But, in any and all cases, do respond to all objections or questions—carefully, thoughtfully, thoroughly, and promptly. Providing the potential giver with all that is needed to make a good decision is a primary responsibility of anyone called to seek gifts in the kingdom.

7. Record.

Once a giving decision is made, it needs to be formalized in writing. Again, it is simply proper stewardship of a gift entrusted to an organization. It may be in the form of a binding pledge or a simple letter of intent. But it should clarify, both for the giver and the organization, the total gift being committed, the period of time and expected intervals of gift payments ($15,000 by [date], given in December of each year). It should also clearly state the intended purpose of the gift so there is no question in the donor's mind of how the gift will be used and no ambiguity from the organization's perspective on how they will utilize these resources. It is often helpful for the document to record if the donors wish to receive regular updates on progress toward fulfillment of the commitment. This gives the organization permission to appropriately remind the donor of their commitment. And, of course, this document should be signed, both by the donor(s) and an officer of the organization. Care on these matters at the point of decision can avert misunderstanding months and years down the road.

> YOU CANNOT APPROPRIATELY RESPOND UNTIL YOU HAVE APPROPRIATELY LISTENED.

8. Thank.

The grace of saying thank you is one that should be cultivated by anyone charged with getting in the kingdom. Your thanks to the donor is a given. You should not only express gratitude personally but in writing as well. In almost every case, a thank-you from the CEO is appropriate, whether or not she has been involved in the gift conversation. But the most important thank-you is from an individual or a group of individuals who benefit from the gift. People *expect* to hear from the development officer and the leader of the organization. But they love to hear from those who directly benefit from their stewardship. For example, providing a modernized classroom in a remote mission school is certainly worthy of attention by the gatherer, as well as the CEO and perhaps even a board member. But for the giver to receive a thank-you from the teacher who utilizes that classroom or, better yet, from the schoolchildren who benefit from the gift every day is a beautiful extension of the grace of saying thank you.

TRANSPARENCY WINS

Sometimes people assume that being the messenger on behalf of the organization to the giver requires knowing all the answers and defending your institution at every turn. Nothing could be more antithetical to a genuine relationship than refusal to acknowledge shortcomings or gaps in our knowledge.

There are two situations in which the temptation is to cover at all costs when, in fact, transparency and utter truthfulness is what the giver expects. In fact, it is needed for a relationship of trust to thrive and for gifts to flow. One situation is when a giver offers criticism or voices concern. The other is when a giver asks a question to which the messenger does not know the answer.

It doesn't matter if you represent an orphanage run by Mother Teresa. Nobody would expect or believe that the operation was beyond reproach. If a giver or prospective giver points out a policy or program (or even person) that does not meet with their approval, there are two possible courses of action. One is to defend at all costs. And, of course, that might be called for in a particular situation. But we have already noted that true givers tend to have a keen insight on human nature, including the human tendencies of our organizations. More often than not, critical questions or outright statements of concern usually touch on a reality for our institution.

The president of my college and I were visiting a person who was keenly interested in making a sizable commitment to endow an important program. We had talked through how the funds would be used over the course of decades. Suddenly, the giver stopped and said, "I have confidence that you will use these funds well during your tenure, but what about after you leave? What confidence can I have that a new president and a new board will honor this commitment?" Thankful that the president was in the room, I looked to him to provide an answer. I was pretty sure he would say something like, "This commitment will be in writing and you can be confident that any new president or board will honor this agreement."

Instead, he said this: "You know, I can't make any ironclad promises about the future. What I can do is point to the century-plus history of this college. That is probably the best I can offer you in terms of the assurances you are asking for."

Silence.

I was thinking, *The least you could say is you have total trust in the process of choosing presidents and board members.* But do you know what? The giver pondered the president's response and said, "You know, I think you're right. Let's go ahead and set this up." I learned an important lesson that day. Instead of "sales-speak" or empty promises, be totally honest and transparent. It is not only the right thing to do, it builds the trust needed for the giver to make investment decisions on your behalf.

The second situation is when the giver asks the gatherer an important question—especially a question that, in hindsight, is something you should have been prepared for! This illustration is as fresh as the last gift conversation I had with a couple. It was about a major remodeling project that would affect a program they had deep interest in. I was pretty proud of the homework I had done. I met with the architect and the campus planner (twice) before the appointment, just to be sure I understood how to describe the plans. I talked with the people who would benefit from the remodeling to get firsthand accounts of what a difference it would make in their program. I talked with the president to make sure he and I were on the same page. Then, as I was going over the plans, they asked a pretty straightforward question: What would be the specific use of the vacated space? Horrors— I didn't know! My first instinct was to make something up! How stupid of me not to have found out! But instead I said something like, "Boy, that is a great question that I should know the answer to, but I don't. Here's what I think, but I will check it out as soon as I get back and let you know." Not knowing the answer was clearly a slipup on my part but at least, on that occasion, I passed the transparency test. And I think that sincerity added to our common reservoir of trust.

> INSTEAD OF "SALES-SPEAK" OR EMPTY PROMISES, BE TOTALLY HONEST AND TRANSPARENT.

Transparency is no cover for an organization's poor preparation or poor performance. But it is the right way to be in seeking gifts in the kingdom.

GIVE CREDIT AWAY—IT ALWAYS COMES BACK

Beware the fundraiser who can tell you how much money they have raised; it probably means they are taking more credit than is appropriate. Think of all the elements and people involved in most gifts. There is the organization and its mission that undoubtedly was the reason for any interest the giver had in the first place. There are often others in the organization who have influenced a giver's love and care for the organization. God has undoubtedly done a work in the lives of the givers to allow them to freely release funds. And who on your team prepared you to ask for the gift? Who faithfully receipted and acknowledged smaller gifts by that same giver over the years? Who had the insight to propose a particular project? Who helped research

> TAKING CREDIT FOR GOD'S ABIDING, GENEROUS WORK ON BEHALF OF YOUR MINISTRY IS UNWORTHY OF SERVICE IN THE KINGDOM.

the proposal? Who offered a prayer for a successful meeting? Taking credit for God's abiding, generous work on behalf of your ministry is unworthy of service in the kingdom. Instead, give credit away. It often comes back.

FUNDRAISERS ARE STEWARDS TOO

The outstanding Christian fundraiser actively calls to careful stewardship those they are privileged to serve—challenging them to weigh financial priorities in light of kingdom values and calling them to be "rich toward God." In fact, the seasoned professional is pretty good at challenging others about what it means to steward their resources. But it is easy to forget that we fundraisers, and the organizations we serve, have the very same obligation under God as the individual giver. The Christian organization, like any follower of Christ, must have an eternal perspective on its work. This life—or more precisely—the life of the organization, from the perspective of eternity, is not the main thing. Christ's kingdom is.

There is another striking similarity between the individual steward and the organization: both are accountable before God for how they use their resources. If that were not enough motivation for organizations to carefully utilize resources entrusted to us, make no mistake—donors care deeply about how the ministries they love and support use their resources. They also care how much of our institutional resources (and theirs!) we use in the process of gathering. There are ways that every church or organization can safeguard its reputation in the way it conducts its work.

1. The board must be the first line of accountability.
It is difficult to imagine an outstanding organization that has not recruited and maintained a strong board. Hiring the senior administrator/pastor, setting policy, inspecting what it expects, and being

the strength and conscience of the organization in good times and bad are what distinguish effective boards from mediocre ones. If the board demands performance and accountability of the organization, that same spirit of accountability will be there within the organization and for its key stakeholders.

2. Calculate the return on investment (ROI) of your efforts to secure financial support.

There is no neat and tidy formula or goal, because every organization is different. A national or international ministry that has a very large constituency with whom they need to keep in frequent contact through direct mail will have a different cost structure than a local organization that relies primarily on a few large gifts. In general, though, ten to twenty cents per dollar raised is a respectable range of expense. Less than 10 percent may indicate you are underresourced in the work of winning friends and financial support. More than 20 percent may indicate inefficiencies or downright sloppiness in your advancement effort. In any case, the genuinely accountable organization will have a grasp on its return on investment and will be willing to share it when asked.

3. Be transparent about the finances of your organization.

There are more ways than ever to demonstrate transparency in how you manage resources entrusted to you. You should make an audited financial statement readily available to anyone who might ask. Very few will ask for it, but your stated willingness to be forthcoming about the financial status of your organization says volumes about your commitment to transparency. Timely filing of IRS form 990 (a requirement of every nonprofit, including individual churches) shows not only to the IRS but also to the public that you are serious about transparency. Your institutional website should have ready access to basic data about your budget, including the sources of revenue and actual categories of expenditures. If we are not willing to make this data known, we are probably not very proud of our own stewardship. An annual report of activities, revenue, and expenditures builds engagement and trust from thoughtful Christian stewards.

For many Christian organizations, the Evangelical Council for Financial Accountability (ECFA) is a suitable and reputable source of financial accreditation. Established in 1979, ECFA "provides accreditation to leading Christian nonprofit organizations that faithfully demonstrate compliance with established standards for financial accountability, fundraising and board governance" (ECFA.org). Members include Christian ministries, denominations, churches, educational institutions, and other tax-exempt 501(c)(3) organizations.

> GIVERS IN THE KINGDOM HAVE THE RIGHT TO EXPECT THAT THE MINISTRIES THEY SUPPORT EXERCISE THE SAME SENSE OF STEWARDSHIP THAT ANIMATES THEIR OWN GIVING.

4. Appearances matter.

No organization can meet everyone's expectation of how it allocates its resources. People's expectations of what is appropriate or adequate—compensation, furnishings, size of staff—is too varied to please everyone. But care for resources entrusted to a church or organization must be obvious in the day-to-day operation of the ministry. It is everyone's responsibility to be as careful in their stewardship of gifts entrusted to them as the giver has been in providing the resources.

Givers in the kingdom have the right to expect that the ministries they support exercise the same sense of stewardship that animates their own giving. If there is a disconnect, our organizations do not deserve to manage their resources. On the other hand, if we make it clear that we share our donors' concerns for careful stewardship, we overcome a major obstacle to support.

VOCATION

I have yet to meet someone involved in getting for the kingdom who at their mother's knee declared, "Mommy, I want to be a fundraiser when I grow up!" And yet, thousands of men and women have answered the call to do just that on behalf of the kingdom. Indeed, the messenger *does* matter. Vocation or calling has been defined by Os Guinness as, "the truth that God calls us to himself so decisively that everything we are, everything we do, and everything we have is invested with a special devotion and dynamism lived out as a response to his summons and service."[14] If gathering resources for kingdom purposes is God's call upon you at this point in your life, you are blessed. Calling God's people to release their resources in service to the kingdom is noble service in that kingdom and worthy of honor. You have opportunity to grow spiritually as you interact with thoughtful givers. You have opportunity to influence obedience to God in the very delicate matter of wealth. And you have opportunity to bring your organization and givers together to accomplish things of eternal significance that would not have happened any other way. If this is your calling, you are blessed, indeed.

CHAPTER

THE **MESSAGE MATTERS**

Words are also actions, and actions are a kind of words.
—Ralph Waldo Emerson

NOTHING NEVER HAPPENS

It was in a college course in linguistics that I learned a life lesson regarding the power of every personal contact to influence the reputation of a person or an organization. The simple lesson was that every human interaction, whether verbal or nonverbal, dramatic or barely perceptible, either adds to or subtracts from a person's storehouse of knowledge and feeling toward the subject. In short, in every human interaction, *nothing **never** happens.* Let me illustrate.

Derek had the privilege of representing a well-respected hospital that has been giving excellent care in the community for generations. Since its founding, the hospital has had a reputation for holistic care of mind, spirit, and body. Its mission is far more than a cold phrase carved in the marble entrance to the hospital. It is the passion of the CEO and her board. It guides hiring and training throughout the institution. Every employee, from the custodial staff to the chief of physicians, could repeat the mission statement by heart.

As chief development officer, Derek had developed a warm relationship with Preston Wells, easily the wealthiest member of the community. Mr. Wells had good reason to care about the continued vibrancy of the hospital because he had experienced it firsthand: once through the marvelous care his mother received in her waning years and, more recently, through the life-saving work of the hospital's medical team in the difficult delivery of his grandson.

All of this made Derek optimistic about his pending meeting with Mr. Wells. But the first meeting with Mr. Wells did not go as well as planned. With some emotion, Preston Wells shared his deep gratitude for the care his mother received in the final month of her life. He was especially grateful for the head nurse, whose name he could not remember, and the doctor who not only checked on his mother every day but also took the time to listen to his mom's needs. He felt just as positive about the care later extended to his daughter and grandson.

> IN EVERY HUMAN INTERACTION, NOTHING NEVER HAPPENS!

There could not have been a better time to ask Mr. Wells for a large gift to the new neonatal center the hospital was contemplating. But once asked, Mr. Wells seemed strangely reluctant to respond. "Why the hesitation?" the befuddled development officer gently probed.

"Frankly," said Mr. Wells, "I'm not convinced you will handle my money well."

"What would make you think that, Mr. Wells?"

"Well, to be honest, the hospital staff doesn't seem competent in the area of money."

"Go on," said Derek, with not a little trepidation.

"For all the good care my mom received, I could not for the life of me decipher her bill. Furthermore," he pressed on, "when I called the accounting office, I was treated—well, frankly—as an interruption. I left messages for a couple of days. When I finally got through (they never did call me back), what I thought of as sincere questions were treated with impatience and dismissiveness. To tell you the truth, I was offended."

"Well," Derek countered hopefully, "even our fine staff can have a bad day."

But Mr. Wells continued. "I thought so too, but I had a similar problem with my daughter's billing from the hospital. As I tried to sort it out, I had the same trouble finding someone to talk to. And when I did, that same irritable tone was evident, even though it was a different person. I was just trying to understand the bill and was treated like I was trying to get away with something. I'm just not sure you will handle my gift with the same care with which I have accumulated it."

Does this story ring true? Might something as small as an unpleasant exchange with an entry-level staff member squelch the impulse to give? I fear it happens more than any of us know: A messy entryway to a building. A gruff word from the parking attendant or a careless error on correspondence. An indiscreet comment overheard. Any of these can undo a world of goodwill and good intention.

In every human interaction, nothing never happens!

What does that mean for any organization? It means that the custodial staff can be as important as the CEO in enhancing the reputation of the organization. The switchboard operator can be as instrumental in attracting a gift to the organization as a presidential visit. The faculty member in the classroom can influence a future alumnus's propensity to give far more than a development officer can. The employee who stops to offer a visitor assistance may seal the trust relationship between a potential donor and the organization. Nothing never happens!

The wise organization incorporates its mission and values in the training and evaluation of every employee. The wise organization does not relegate service to the development office alone! When every member of the organization assumes responsibility to represent its core values to all who come in contact with the organization, getting gifts becomes more natural and less contrived.

A few years ago I visited the campus of Washington and Lee University. After walking around a bit, I noticed that *every* student I passed on the sidewalk greeted me with, "Hello sir," or a similar greeting. I was taken with it. When I got to the development office, I made a comment about my surprise and delight with this unsolicited response. The development officer smiled and said, "It is a longtime tradition among our students. They joyfully carry on the tradition, student generation after student generation," he told me, "and you wouldn't believe how it strengthens our hand in relationships with donors. In fact," he went on to say, "once, a visitor came to campus and was so moved by the students' warm reception that he gave a significant unsolicited gift to the university. He told us that any university with students of this character deserved his support!" Nothing never happens.

THE MISSION IS CENTRAL

Clarity of mission could be the most important differential between the effective organization and the mediocre one. Philanthropic causes, whether inside or outside the kingdom, are launched by the moral imperative to meet an unmet need. Mission clearly and succinctly identifies that need. It may be hunger or ignorance or drug abuse or disease. But mission does not describe the *programs* utilized to address the moral or social ill. Mission answers the question, "Why do we exist?" The answer to that question, for any organization, is the central reference point for any organization. It gives birth to specific programs that address the fundamental concern.

Why is mission so important? In the matter of giving and getting, clarity of mission is crucial. People only support what they understand. And fundraising devoid of mission and purpose is mercenary and unworthy of service in the kingdom. Organizations are not the only entities with missions, either. People have them too. They may call them personal passions or lifelong interests, but they constitute what is important to the giver in the context of the kingdom. It is when the mission and passion of the organization match the mission and purpose of the giver that extraordinary giving happens. If we cannot declare with certitude and clarity what we are about, and if we cannot help identify that same passion in the individual, giving and getting do not happen.

Quick: As a gatherer for your organization, how would you describe the mission? Is there a formal statement? Have you memorized it? Is it known not just by gatherers but by the custodial

> IN THE MATTER OF GIVING AND GETTING, CLARITY OF MISSION IS CRUCIAL.

staff, the board members, and the people you serve? Are you sure? Does it state why you exist, not what you do? Does it differentiate you appropriately from other organizations that do similar work? How? Why?

Being crystal clear about your mission is empowering. It enables the messenger to go with confidence before any potential giver. It fortifies your courage to ask and the integrity to receive. It helps the organization decide what to do. And, perhaps just as important, it helps the organization decide what not to do!

Beware of mission drift. It usually comes about through competence gained in pursuing the mission. Drift begins like this: "We're good at this, so why not try that?" "We are called to deliver shelter to abused women, so maybe we should provide legal advocacy for those victims." Of course that may be a wonderful expansion of your central mission. But the wise organization will look long and hard to decide if a new initiative is a natural extension of its central mission or the first step toward mission drift and lack of clarity for those who are called to support your mission. Mission could not be more central to the process of giving and getting in the kingdom. Know it and live it—every day and in every interaction.

THE MESSAGE MUST CORRELATE WITH REALITY

What we say about the mission and work of our organizations must match the reality in which we find ourselves. Vision and faith are inspiring to those called to give. But they must be rooted in a sober assessment of the situation and capabilities of the organization. The balance is tricky to be sure. Being bound in vision by what is currently feasible and affordable is a recipe for mediocrity. Dollars don't reward extreme caution and conservatism. But neither do they chase expansive plans that don't correlate with the organization's economic reality. One of the primary responsibilities of delivering the organization's message is to lead thinking and change within a context that recognizes the times and circumstances. If the message does not correspond with an objective view of reality, gifts will not, and perhaps, should not come. A vision for a way forward, while recognizing potential obstacles, will inspire confidence—and gifts.

CHAPTER 8

THE **DONOR/INVESTOR**
MATTERS **MOST**

I used to ask donors about the stock market and their business.
Now I ask about their children and their grandchildren.

—Veteran fundraiser

PUT AWAY THE TIN CUP

By far the most common shorthand description of the task of fundraising is "begging for money." That description is born, in part, of ignorance. Many people have not thought through the issues addressed in this book: God's ownership of all we possess, the moral imperative to give, the eternal value of investing in the kingdom, and intrinsic rewards of voluntary action for the greater good. Anyone with the mind-set that their resources are theirs and theirs alone would naturally be offended by the temerity of someone asking them to give some of those resources away. The irritation we feel at the imposition of the street beggar shaking a tin cup in our hearing is easily transposed to anyone and any organization seeking a donation.

On the other hand, some of the reputation of fundraising as begging is well earned. Many organizations, board members, and not a few men and women involved in the process of securing resources for the organization approach the task in just this way. Requests for support appeal to immediate need ("Please help us finish the year in the black" or "Please help us achieve our campaign goal") rather than asking for an investment in a noble cause. We send letters and brochures rather than initiate conversations. We hint instead of asking. We wish more than we plan. Why is this so?

We may have lost passion for our mission. We may have lapsed into a maintenance mode rather than generating big ideas related to our mission. Or we may be consumed with the fear of rejection. Whatever the reason, if we lead with the tin cup when we have the resources to think and plan and thoughtfully ask, we do the giver a disservice. Evaluate every letter, every brochure, every new program, and every conversation. Have you fallen back on the easier path of begging and hoping with tin cup in hand, or have you pursued the more difficult but more fruitful work of engaging every potential giver? True givers deserve thoughtful engagement. If you have more resources than a tin cup, put it away!

> HAVE YOU FALLEN BACK ON THE EASIER PATH OF BEGGING AND HOPING WITH TIN CUP IN HAND, OR HAVE YOU PURSUED THE MORE DIFFICULT BUT MORE FRUITFUL WORK OF ENGAGING EVERY POTENTIAL GIVER?

LISTEN BEFORE YOU SPEAK

Every giver has the right to be heard. We know that very few gifts are given from the wallet to the organization without worldview, sense of stewardship, and empathy entering mightily in the decision. Too often our approach to individuals conveys a lack of concern for their passion and point of view. Giving in the kingdom is too important for the gatherer to talk without first listening.

Why is it difficult to listen before we speak? Organizations and their representatives have a lot to say. We are thoroughly immersed in the work we do. The life of any organization is a constant stream of intense board discussions, planning sessions, position papers, programs, and program evaluations. No one knows the challenges or the potential nearly as well as we do. Besides, the giver has willingly come to our event or invited us into their home or office. Of course they want to hear all we have to say!

The thoughtful giver may be too kind to demand more, but they deserve more. If we are truly honoring the God-given interests, passions, and resources of the giver, we will listen before we speak. What do they care about? What has consumed their time and attention in recent days? What do they love about your cause? Why are they interested at all? What disappoints them about the work your organization does? What do they wish you did better?

These and similar questions are not the "setup" for the ask. For the giver and getter alike, this conversation sets the context from which joyful gifts can be given with confidence. Is there some risk in listening before we talk? Of course. We relinquish total control of the conversation. We make ourselves and our organizations more vulnerable than we might otherwise be. But the upside is far more rewarding, for the relationship and, potentially, for the organization. When we listen well, we learn how the organization is actually perceived rather than being captured by our own narrative of how we *want* to be perceived. We gain new ideas. We are forced to sharpen our message (mission, project, and specific appeal). We have treated a fellow citizen of the kingdom with the honor they deserve. And more often than not, we have gained a partner rather than a patron in our important work. Be intentional. Listen before you speak. Your discipline and care for others will be rewarded.

DO YOUR HOMEWORK

Be prepared. A tangible way we can honor the giver is to do our homework well before any significant interaction. The work of getting in the kingdom is about 90 percent grunt work and 10 percent glory!

From the outside, people see the work of the getter (except of course for the important detail of asking for the gift) as exciting and even fun. Travel, meetings at country clubs or fine homes, and interesting people are all part of the work. But the work we engage in before and after these "events" is what distinguishes contacts from relationships and gifts from investments.

Before the meeting.

There are likely many possibilities available to you as you gather information to enhance the value of your individual contact with the giver. They revolve around points of connection with your organization, family, and establishing a tentative goal for the contact.

First, what are the points of connection to your organization? For most individuals, there is a trail, either recorded data or institutional memory, of contact information that will reveal when a relationship began, high (and low) points of the relationship, lulls in the relationship, and giving history (we will discuss the importance of planning and record keeping in chapter 9). Granted, you can breeze into a conversation and declare, "Hey, I'm new here. Tell me about your relationship with us." But it is much better to have taken the time to assemble a picture of that person's relationship with the organization. You will honor them by investing this time, and you will have laid the groundwork for a deeper and more meaningful relationship.

HAVE AN OBJECTIVE FOR EVERY CONTACT, WHETHER A CALL OR AN INDIVIDUAL MEETING.

Another part of your preparation is being aware of the giver's family. Who are the members of the immediate family? What are their names? Do they have children? If grown, where do they live? Are other members of their extended family involved with your organization? Have other generations of the family been involved with you? Has that involvement enhanced or detracted from their relationship with you? Being prepared with family information and awareness of family concerns demonstrates genuine care for the donor.

A final and crucial point of preparation for a meeting is to determine an objective for the meeting. The time and attention of the giver is a gift in itself. Are you prepared to make that expenditure of time on their part a valuable one? Even the most casual appointment or conversation has great potential to move a relationship forward. Remember, nothing never happens (chapter 7). Have an objective for every contact, whether a call or an individual meeting. Is it to say thank you? Is it to provide an update on the work of the organization? Is it to discover the giver's willingness and capacity to give? Is it to ask permission to ask (chapter 6)? Is it to present a specific proposal? Is it a follow-up on a proposed giving decision? Pointless or overly general objectives for a meeting might qualify as a "contact," but relationships rarely move forward without intentionality.

After the meeting.

There are few significant interactions with givers that do not call for more homework. Sometimes it is only seizing the opportunity to say "thank you." After all, they invested time for the interaction. A written thank-you is a small but important gesture of appreciation and friendship. But often there is more: a lingering question that could not be answered at the meeting; a proposal that needs to be refined; a lead to another interested giver that needs to be followed. This is where the true work of a meaningful relationship takes place. And it requires personal and institutional commitment to fulfill. Carving out time for prior preparation and the meeting itself is a significant commitment. But without follow-up, those efforts are in large measure wasted. A commitment ignored, even one as seemingly trivial as the answer to a mundane question, may be a blip on the screen to the getter but a quiet and significant disappointment to the giver that could cost your organization dearly. Doing your homework well will distinguish your organization in the mind of the giver and will honor the true value of the giver to your work.

DEFY PRECONCEPTIONS/EXCEED EXPECTATIONS

Experience teaches us and research confirms: true givers almost invariably support between ten and twenty charitable causes. That has many implications for how organizations relate to givers, but we will focus on just one now. While from the organization's perspective, we are dealing with a singular relationship, from the giver's perspective, we may be one of many similar relationships. It stands to reason, then, that how you manage preconceptions and expectations will make a huge difference in the quality and depth of relationship.

Preconceptions.

It's time for some realistic self-evaluation. Human nature is predisposed to categorizing the work of those whose vocation it is to gather funds. What are some of those categories? "More interested in my money than me." "Salesman." "Flatterer." Or, to put it in Emily Dickinson's clever terms, "Fundraisers are people who impose themselves on me and then tell all the truth, but tell it slant." The sad news is that caricatures will persist. That is because of the human nature of the giver and the getter! But every gatherer on behalf of the kingdom has it within them to break harmful preconceptions by defying them with a principled, godly life. Consistently operating with authenticity, reliability, and crystal integrity will quickly dispel unfortunate stereotypes. And, of course, a lapse in any of these will quickly place us back in the pack of well-meaning but unreliable messengers. How we conduct ourselves is totally within our control. It can distinguish us from other giving/getting relationships and result in meaningful and productive associations with those who can alter the course of our organizations. Preconceptions can be quietly altered by a principled life.

Expectations.

Then there is the matter of expectations. Most true givers expect from the giver/getter relationship what they expect from any healthy relationship. The list of expectations is not that long, but it is important: honesty, punctuality, responsiveness, preparedness, and a loving, caring spirit. I don't know anyone, inside or outside the kingdom, who does not consider these expectations reasonable. Beware of the insidious circumstances that draw us away from consistently living out those expectations. Often it is simply busyness that causes us to take our eye off the ball of our own expectations. If it persists, we are probably trying to be too many things to too many people. Perhaps we need to give way to others who can provide the care true givers deserve. Exceeding expectations is not a technique for raising more money. It is what is required of faithful service in Christ's kingdom.

GROW THE GIVER

He is an extraordinary giver and has come to be a genuine friend. He is also one of the most accomplished and gracious businessmen I have ever met. Years ago he shared a story with me that changed how I thought about the work of getting in the kingdom. "I'm a very busy person," he began, "but the nature of our business is that we have many vendors we rely upon to arrive at our finished product. A lot of them try to see me. One day, after meeting with a sales representative, a question occurred to me: Why do I always agree to an appointment with this person? I would normally deflect someone who sells at his level to someone else in my company. Why do I take the appointment myself?"

"I'll tell you why," he continued. "It's because he always has something interesting to say. It might be a recent article he read that relates to an issue in our industry. It might be an insight on a family matter I have confided to him. It might be an interesting anecdote about my favorite sports team. Anytime I talk with him on the phone or meet with him in my office, I learn something. I grow as a businessman and a person. No wonder I always take time for him."

> **FOR GIVERS TO BE INTERESTED IN MEETING WITH US, WE NEED TO BE INTERESTING PEOPLE.**

The lesson is obvious. For givers to be interested in meeting with us, we need to be interesting people. Not witty or even wise. Just cultivate in yourself the desire to be an interesting person who is well-read, observant, and considerate. Early in my career I determined that, despite my natural interests, I would read the *Wall Street Journal* and the *New York Times* every day. It was a huge stepping-stone in being more aware of my world and the world of the givers with whom I would interact.

Beyond being interesting and engaging, we have a platform to help all those we meet with grow in their understanding of what it means to invest treasure, "where moth and rust [do not] destroy, and where thieves [do not] break in and steal" (Matthew 6:19). What could be more satisfying or ultimately important than helping God's people understand that, "Where your treasure is, there will your heart be also" (Matthew 6:21)? A gatherer in the kingdom should have the capacity and desire to grow the giver. That honors the giver and deepens their joy and resolve to invest generously and strategically in the kingdom.

— PART III —
FUNDRAISING:
A WAY OF DOING

God is looking for people through whom
He can do the impossible—what a pity that we plan
only the things we can do by ourselves.

—A.W. TOZER

CHAPTER

THE HALLMARKS
OF A STRONG PROGRAM

---

*The only things that evolve by themselves in an organization
are disorder, friction and malperformance.*
—Peter F. Drucker

Every organization is different. They are shaped by their histories and traditions, the unique nature of their work, their leadership, their constituencies, and the people filling particular roles within them. Nonetheless, there are elements common to effective, principled fundraising programs. To be the best at our particular God-given task, it is helpful to emulate proven, exceptional ways of gathering resources from careful stewards in the kingdom. It is to those hallmarks of a strong program that we now turn our attention.

THE BEST FUNDRAISERS SERVE
We have already said this in many ways, but it bears repeating. Those whose privilege it is to gather must possess a passion to serve. You can prepare well, present well, converse well, write well, and follow-up well, but if your primary orientation is not to serve well, you will fail at the task of getting in the kingdom.

The gifted gatherer serves the organization. Your important role in funding the work of the organization is not God's gift to the organization; the organization is God's gift to you. With all of its shortcomings, the organization you serve is dedicated to meeting human needs for the sake of the kingdom. And you get to spend your vocational energy advancing that eternal purpose.

What does it mean to serve the organization? It means recognizing and appreciating that institutional resources are not there for your benefit but are ultimately to be harnessed in service to the mission. It requires making good use of time on behalf of the organization. Contacting one more potential donor a day can make the difference between adequate and exemplary service. Extraordinary service means taking the time and effort to know your organization intimately, not just the funding goals and mission of the organization but its people and its potential. Such knowledge enables you to deliver information, passion, and stories to the potential giver that will genuinely connect him or her to the organization. That depth of commitment and service to the organization is winsome to the giver and worthy of its eternally significant mission. But genuine service to the organization that is not translated into genuine service to individual givers lies outside the standards of the kingdom. Jesus Himself came "not to be served, but to serve" (Matthew 20:28). What does it mean to serve givers?

> IF YOUR PRIMARY ORIENTATION IS NOT TO SERVE WELL, YOU WILL FAIL AT THE TASK OF GETTING IN THE KINGDOM.

Relate to them as whole people, not wealthy potential benefactors.

Giver and getter alike need to be intentional about genuine relationships. From the getter's point of view, look at all the factors that pull you away from genuine relationship and toward salesmanship. Your primary responsibility to your organization is to secure resources. You might be in the middle of a campaign or at the end of a fiscal year where immediate commitments appear much more valuable than future commitments. You have personal expectations of your performance, and so does your organization. The giver may have the view (sometimes well-founded) that the only reason an organization's development officer would visit is to secure a gift. Or perhaps the giver's primary link is to the organization and its mission, not to any particular getter.

The way to overcome these challenges is not to pretend that giving is not part of the relationship equation. It is a given that must be managed. Neither the giver nor the getter should cultivate a relationship that does not include as its primary focus the well-being of the organization. But caring first for the *person*, and placing others' needs above your own, is true service. Sitting with a grieving friend and quietly sharing her grief may be just the service you are called to perform. Telling her about your institution's memorial gift program may not be! Seeking genuine ways to serve those related to your ministry is not only the right thing to do, it is proof that you and your organization value people and relationships more than gifts.

Help them see their part in the success of your organization.

One of the ways a gatherer can serve the giver is to help her understand how her friendship, prayers, and financial support strengthen your organization. After all, the giver's involvement, at whatever level, indicates an investment in you for the sake of the kingdom. So tell him: "Here is why your $1 million gift was transformational for us. Here are other gifts that it leveraged by example. This is what your $15 per month for the past twelve years means to us. Your act of regular stewardship, accompanied by your prayers and best wishes, encourages and strengthens us in ways that you cannot fully know."

When we are faithful in helping the thoughtful Christian steward know what difference their investment in us is making, we validate their investment of time, as well as spiritual and financial capital. We also serve them and their primary interest, rather than "servicing" a client. There is a world of difference between the two. Givers know the difference, and so does the Lord of the kingdom.

Grow them as people and stewards.

The getter has the great privilege of helping God's people grow both in their thinking about giving and in the exercise of generous giving itself. How can we serve the giver toward that end? We can share stories. People love to hear how the organization they love has been impacted by other givers, whether a crinkled $5 bill from a prison inmate touched by the organization, or the couple who stretched mightily to provide the decisive gift in the campaign. Stories enliven the imagination of the giver to envision how their stewardship can be meaningful in the expansion of Christ's kingdom.

We can also ask for commitment. If done appropriately, and at the appropriate time, *we* can become the instrument that enables a giver to grow in the joy of releasing resources for eternal purposes. Yes, asking for a gift can be an act of service to the giver. Absolutely! The joy and satisfaction donors feel in giving when asked is often palpable. Sometimes they shed tears of joy; sometimes they offer verbal expressions of gratitude for the ability to give. Sometimes an unmistakably satisfied countenance reveals an inner peace and sense of "rightness" in responding affirmatively to an invitation to give for a specific purpose. Telling and asking are ways the getter can, indeed, serve the thoughtful Christian steward. Scripture, in the context of service in the church, says, "Those who have served well gain an excellent standing and great assurance in their faith in Jesus Christ" (1 Timothy 3:13). Giving in the kingdom is one of the ways a disciple of Christ can serve well.

THE BEST LEADERS KNOW THEIR PLACE

I have served three presidents and observed or counseled many others. They certainly share common features: high energy, intelligence, and deep dedication to the success of the organizations they serve. But in the matter of getting financial resources, there can be huge differences. Some love the task and can hardly wait to get to it. Others see their role as vision casters but blanche at or even disdain asking for the gift. I would argue that the "place" of the president/CEO, or pastor, in leading the fundraising effort of their organization is both front and center *and* quietly in the background, regardless of their giftedness and interests. Let me explain.

First, the president/CEO or pastor is, without exception, the chief development officer of their organization. Wait. What about the executive pastor? What about the chief advancement officer? Aren't they responsible for that? Well, in a sense, yes. But not ultimately. What is required for meaningful support of any organization? Sound leadership, fiscal accountability, mission centeredness, vision casting, and winning friends and financial support. A leader needs assistance in all these areas but can never delegate the ultimate responsibility for any of them to others. The leader of the organization sets the tone for all—within and outside the organization. The "place" of the CEO is front and center.

But the place of the leader is also often quietly (though never passively) in the background. Remember what we said about the number of relationships that any one person can manage well (chapter 4)? A president or senior pastor is pulled in many directions, and everyone in the church or organization assumes a certain access to them. This is natural and, to some degree, necessary. But it presents a big problem if it diverts attention away from the important work of getting resources.

That is why it is essential to have a person or division of people responsible for gift development. Their job is to weigh resources available for funding operational and aspirational needs. What is the vision of the president and board? Who are your current givers? Who are past but lapsed givers? Who should know about your organization and have a stake in your future? Who are key stakeholders that justify the time and attention of the president in relation to their *stewardship* (everyone is a key stakeholder in terms of their other involvements in the organization)?

A leader must serve the development team in several important ways. The first way to serve is to hold the development team accountable for performance. While giving is affected by myriad forces, it is also measurable, as is the activity employed to secure deeper and broader participation in the life of the organization.

The second way the president or senior pastor can serve the development team is to transfer his or her own credibility to the development team. If you trust the heart and competence of your development team, one of the best ways you can empower them is to convey your trust in them to current and prospective givers. The equation goes something like this: if a person trusts you, the leader, then they will most likely be responsive to the person in your organization in whom you demonstrate trust. This frees you, the president or senior pastor, from many of the more detailed aspects of the giving relationship. That is how wise presidents, pastors, and ministry leaders serve the greatest number of stakeholders in their orbit. The leader who insists on being a part of every step of every giving relationship will let too many things drop and will end up doing disservice to the individual and the institution. The leader who simply abdicates the task of getting likewise does a disservice to the individual and the institution. The leader who casts the vision for all, manages giving relationships with a few, and actively delegates most giving relationships to the development team ends up serving the most people in the best way.

The development team bears a great deal of responsibility for helping the president or senior pastor succeed. Discernment of when to engage the president with the giver is critical. If the president is the only one who can cast the vision, ask for the gift, or thank for the gift from a particular donor, then the development team should make sure the president deals with the issue directly. If the president is not directly crucial to an issue, the development team needs to take the responsibility to make things happen. A competent development team member should live with the healthy fear of this question from the CEO: "Why exactly did you need me to be at that meeting?" I hate that question! The leader who steps up whenever required, and steps back whenever appropriate, serves the organization and its people best.

THE BEST BOARDS SUPPORT THE FUNDRAISING TEAM

The adage in the business world about the role of the board in support of its president goes something like this: "Our job at every board meeting is to ask two questions of the CEO (or vice president if a committee meeting), 'Should we fire him?' and, if not, 'How can we help him succeed?'" Not a bad shorthand for the assessment role of the board. Assessment is a critical aspect of governing the development program of any organization. How are resources being utilized? What is the return on investment (ROI) in the development area? Are development staff productive? Are the programs innovative, growing, and reaching the entire constituency? Are resources adequate? These questions, while sometimes uncomfortable to ask or answer, represent the kind of accountability that is appropriate in managing resources committed to kingdom work.

If these questions have been satisfactorily addressed, then the question of how the board can come alongside the development effort becomes relevant. There are many tangible ways boards as a whole and individual board members can encourage and enable the difficult work of securing resources. One way is in corporate and individual giving. (We address this in chapter 12.) Boards who lead the way in generous support of the organization strengthen the development effort in significant ways. They give getters more courage to ask and givers more reason to give.

Another way board members can support the work of development is to use their personal talents and spheres of influence on behalf of the organization. *All* board members can give. Some board members have the ability to ask; those who can do so are most likely generous givers themselves who can speak with conviction to other potential givers about the importance of their gifts. These board members possess personality and understanding to call others to commitment. While it may take someone on the development team to see this potential and ask for it, this resource must not be overlooked.

Other board members, while perhaps not well suited to ask, can do a superb job of telling. Rather than having a paid person (the president or development officer) tell others why they should support the institution, it is much more powerful for a volunteer (board member) to share why they give generously of their time, talent, and treasure to your cause. Telling the story from an insider's perspective is a marvelous way to support the development effort.

A third way board members can support their organization in getting resources is to engage others in their particular area of influence. This is not preying on others if it is approached thoughtfully and discriminately. The question is not, "Who do I know who has money and owes me something?" but "Who do I know whose animating passions would mesh well with the mission of this institution?" Inviting a true giver to consider if your particular organization would be an appropriate outlet is not an imposition; it is an opportunity for service. Again, attitudes and prejudices about getting in the kingdom can make us timid in our responsibility to engage people to advance the kingdom. Done well, the person we bring to the table will thank us for the opportunity, whether or not they end up as donors to our cause.

THE BEST FUNDRAISING TEAMS PULL TOGETHER

Your development effort may consist of the CEO teaming with one director of development, one marketing person, and one gift receipter; or it may be a full-fledged advancement division of a hundred people with departments of development, annual fund drive, planned giving, marketing, and advancement services. Regardless, the best programs approach their work as a team rather than competitors. In the flow of activity of gathering resources, there are natural milestones: the completion of an annual fund goal, the introduction of a new website or publication, the completion of a comprehensive campaign, the implementation of a new system to track and receipt gifts, or the receipt of the largest gift in the history of the organization. All of these events represent a singular accomplishment attained by a team effort.

The best programs celebrate and acknowledge the efforts of the entire team. Think of the travel program of the organization that netted a large gift from someone who was able to see firsthand the compassion and effectiveness of your organization. She may have handed the check to your president. But someone other than the CEO conceived the travel program in the first place. Someone else managed the logistics of the travel in a way that pleased every participant. There were many people associated with your organization who were doing the work of your organization in the presence of the donor. There were folks back home who had faithfully and accurately receipted scores of gifts from this giver over many years. And there was a major gifts officer who had genuinely loved and served this individual over many years and had, in fact, invited her to attend the trip.

In this and hundreds of similar examples, it is often the combined efforts of many people over many years that eventuate into a specific gift. The more all members of the team see their place as important to the overall effort, whether they are on the front lines or unseen, the more the development effort points away from any one individual to the One for whom the work is done. That is pulling together in the development task. That reflects the true character of getting in the kingdom.

> THE BEST PROGRAMS APPROACH THEIR WORK AS A TEAM RATHER THAN COMPETITORS.

THE BEST VOLUNTEERS LOVE THE CAUSE
MORE THAN THE RESPONSIBILITY

Volunteers are a potential treasure for any nonprofit. They represent all that is right about giving and getting in the kingdom. They give not only financial resources but also what, for some, are scarcer commodities: time and energy. Allowing stakeholders to be actively involved demonstrates an organization's transparency and care for the giver. It has the potential to propel the organization forward while deepening relationships, all in a cost-effective way. But involving volunteers, like everything else in the process of getting, requires intentionality and care.

The dictionary definition of volunteer is "a person who performs a service willingly and without pay." Making volunteer service satisfying for the individual and the organization requires a good bit of work on the part of the organization. Organizations make two common mistakes with volunteers. One is failing to plan well. The other is to not discriminate in choosing volunteers.

Success with volunteers takes almost as much work as success with paid employees. Someone in the organization needs to be formally responsible for selecting, training, and supervising volunteers. Inviting volunteers without a job description, written expectations, and—yes—the ability to relieve them of their duties if they fail to perform is a recipe for frustration and failure.

Volunteers can provide basic service, such as stuffing envelopes, or they can be co-laborers in saying thank you or even asking others to contribute to the cause. One couple I know, alumni of a Christian college, quietly and painstakingly handwrite nearly three hundred condolence cards every year to other alumni who have lost loved ones. They've been doing it for years. Their own personal experience and the care they bring to the notes serve the college in a way that could not be duplicated by any paid staff member. From construction expertise at a camp to *pro bono* legal services at a social service agency to welcoming patients at a hospital, volunteers who are carefully selected, guided, and thanked can extend the influence and efficiency of any organization while providing meaningful ways to serve.

The second common mistake organizations make in regard to volunteers is to not be discriminating in recruitment. Casting the net wide ("whoever wants to help, please show up") can be poor stewardship on the part of the organization. You would never hire just anyone who wanted to work in your employ. The best programs identify people with the disposition and ability to contribute to the organization, and recruit them to serve. Many of the dynamics of asking for a gift apply to asking for volunteers. It requires knowledge of the passions of the potential volunteer. It requires their understanding of and love for the culture and mission of the organization. And it often involves a call for their commitment to service. Busy, capable people have many claims upon their time. Intentionality and discernment in recruiting volunteers can serve the organization and the giver alike, all for the benefit of the kingdom.

THE BEST PROGRAMS

What are the characteristics that differentiate highly effective development programs from the merely adequate ones? The best programs:

Plan well.

Development work is difficult not only because it involves relating to many people, all with different levels of interest, but because it is labor/planning intensive. People who do not understand the task may imagine nice receptions and airplane trips and meeting with interesting people—all true, of course. But experience shows that good development work is about 90 percent planning and about 10 percent execution. That's 90 percent grunt work and 10 percent glory!

> THE WORK OF GETTING IN THE KINGDOM IS ABOUT 90 PERCENT GRUNT WORK AND 10 PERCENT GLORY!

Many years ago I heard a seasoned development professional say, "God don't sponsor no flops!" I think what he was saying is that the stakes in asking God's people for God's money for God's work are pretty high. And it takes a great deal of planning and discernment to do justice to the process and to the thoughtful stewards we seek to engage.

It is relatively easy to draft a letter describing a project that needs to be funded, as is asking for a gift in that letter. But determining who should receive the letter and who shouldn't, when it should be sent, and a cost-effective way to get the letter out takes no small amount of planning. And should everyone get the same letter, regardless of their ability to give, how recently they last gave a gift, etc.?

Direct mail is a relatively small aspect of most development programs. How about planning the next step with a major giving prospect? Writing a proposal to a foundation or corporation? Creating a program and invitation list for a focused event? Researching the estate consequences of a major gift? Deciding when to launch a campaign, and for what purpose and with what financial goal, and on what time line? Planning is one of the most important functions in any program designed to win friends and resources to a cause. The greatest strides are made by organizations with the ability to plan well and the discipline to carry out that plan.

Ask well.

The premise of this book is that to call Christian men and women to commitment of their resources in service to the kingdom is a noble undertaking. Asking is not, in and of itself, noble. But careful, thoughtful, prayerful engagement of God's people for the sake of God's work in this world defines what it means to be a gatherer in Christ's kingdom. Asking cannot be careless or indiscriminate. How is it that the best programs consistently ask well?

They are more attentive to the giver's needs than their own. The easy thing to do is to ask when our needs require it: when the timetable of our campaign or the end of our fiscal year demands, or (worst of all) when the getter needs a gift to justify a trip or fill out a report! But a gift request, bereft of relationship and preparation, is a violation of the trust necessary between the giver and the getter. In the course of an ongoing conversation about the organization, its mission, and its immediate opportunities, it is the timing and disposition of the giver that matters most. As we have said in many ways, listening is the discipline that helps reveal when it is appropriate to ask. Letting the giver's needs direct the conversation may not fit into our timetable, but it provides the best opportunity for a joyful, generous gift.

> PLANNING IS ONE OF THE MOST IMPORTANT FUNCTIONS IN ANY PROGRAM DESIGNED TO WIN FRIENDS AND RESOURCES TO A CAUSE.

They plan carefully. Asking for and receiving a gift is rarely a spontaneous event. It involves careful assessment of readiness and capacity to give. Asking for a gift of $1,000 from a person with the capacity (and latent desire) to give $100,000 signals lack of preparation and wisdom and will probably garner the smaller gift. But knowing what animates a passion for giving and having a sense of what size gift will reflect that passion is what separates intentional programs from the perfunctory. Time constraints, fear of rejection, and uncertainty about the timing of the ask all conspire to make what could be a gift commitment into a mere appointment on a calendar. Planning well honors the giver and enables the release of more resources for kingdom purposes.

When the time appears right, they ask. You have established a meaningful relationship with a couple. You have discerned the animating passion for their giving of time, talent, and treasure. You have researched and answered their questions and suggestions. You have asked permission to ask. What remains? The ask. I don't know anyone who is totally comfortable with asking for financial commitment. That is as it should be. I would be nervous about anyone who is casual and comfortable in treading into such unknown and sacred space as a person's deepest passion for contributing to God's work. But with prayer and planning and courage, getting in the kingdom most often requires that we ask. A gentle, thoughtful, firm ask. I can't remember leaving my car for such an appointment without breathing this prayer: "Lord, this conversation has potential to make a big difference for my organization and Your kingdom. I'm not going in there without You." The best programs plan well and ask well.

They recognize that the yes is not the end of the effort, but the beginning of a deeper relationship. Beware the huge temptation to see the yes as the realization of your objective with the giver. Think about it. Your organization is counting on you. You've got a plan. You have done the important leg work. The gift is a huge benefit to your cause. The project can go forward. The human response is relief and the opportunity to enjoy and rest. But the best programs resist that impulse. Honoring the giver beyond the gift is natural if you prize the perspective of the giver. While a gift may be the culmination of months or years of effort on the part of the getter, it is an important marker in the life of the careful steward. What lies ahead for the giver? Fulfilling the commitment. Following their investment with the great interest that our Lord predicted ("Where your treasure

> **THE BEST MINISTRIES PUT AS MUCH EFFORT AND RESOURCES IN STEWARDING THE GIFT AFTER IT IS GIVEN AS SEEKING THE GIFT IN THE FIRST PLACE.**

is, there will your heart be also"). And it involves evaluating if their stewardship is paying the dividends in the kingdom as they anticipated. The best ministries put as much effort and resources into stewarding the gift after it is given as seeking the gift in the first place.

Thank well.

What does it mean to thank well? If giving is rooted in grace, then thanking well is reasonable service in the kingdom. Thanking well is not just a way to cultivate a future gift. It is a gracious response to a gracious gift. Thanking well has several characteristics.

It is timely. A gift of any size may be a regular occurrence in the organization. But make no mistake, it is a thoughtful and significant event for the giver. Most givers have no overt *need* for recognition. Their motives almost always are related to eternal values, not immediate reward. But to acknowledge a gift in a timely fashion reinforces the urgency of your request for the gift and demonstrates care for the giver. One organization has a policy: they don't deposit a gift until they have said thank you for that gift! That communicates a high standard of care and a high view of the giver of every gift.

It is sincere. Sincerity, by its very nature, cannot be manufactured. So how do you ensure sincere gratitude? By recognizing—every time—that a gift is not a matter of course. It is a divine transaction in which a follower of Christ determines that God's call on his or her life is a specific investment in His kingdom. The amount has no effect on the importance of this divine transaction. If it is given in obedience and joyful obligation, the gift is an event of spiritual and eternal significance.

It is frequent and varied. Thank you is not a onetime event. Neither is it relegated to the immediate receiver of the gift. Gratitude should be deep and wide. The getter is grateful, of course, for the act of giving itself. It is the culmination of a process. But from the giver's perspective, it is much more. The giver didn't give to make the day or meet the quota of the gatherer! She gave to help accomplish God's work through your organization. So how can the *organization* say thank you meaningfully?

> IT IS NECESSARY FOR THE ORGANIZATION TO COMMIT RESOURCES TO ENSURE THAT IT EXCELS IN THE GRACE OF SAYING THANK YOU.

This question requires immense care and intentionality on the part of the organization. Who benefits from the gift? The gift may have been given to provide competent legal counsel for those without the financial ability to defend themselves. In that case, who can and should say "thank you"? The gatherer? Sure. The CEO responsible for the entire process? Of course.

But how about an expression of thanks from the person who was enabled through release time to provide the legal service?

How about a handwritten note from the single mom who received justice because of the gift? These are the expressions of thanks that mean the most because they reflect the true reason for the gift.

But human nature being what it is, it is necessary for the organization to commit resources to ensure that it excels in the grace of saying thank you. While everyone's responsibility in every organization is to be gracious and thankful, some of the best organizations allocate resources for the position of Coordinator of Donor Care, or something similar. That person's responsibility is to be an extra set of eyes and hands to make sure the organization is intentional about thanking frequently, with variety, and well. And "thank you" is not just for when the gift happens.

Gratitude should be expressed over the expanse of time that the gift is serving its purpose.

That is a much higher bar and requires organizational intentionality. Getting is far more than receiving. It is saying "thank you" well.

It is an attitude as much as an act. In the best programs, thankfulness is not a program but rather an attitude emanating from a grateful spirit. It must be modeled by the organization's leadership and board. It must be practiced by all who touch the lives of givers. It must be reinforced by sharing stories of God's provision through His people. It is possible to cultivate a spirit of gratitude. Our Lord commended it. And giving ourselves to excellence in service to the kingdom demands it.

Evaluate well.

In the delicate matter of interaction with those who love and care for your cause, the best programs are meticulous about reflection and evaluation. It is easy to conclude after a successful large event or individual meeting with a giver or prospective giver, "That went well." It's tempting to make that the extent of our evaluation. Certainly events or individual meetings that clearly fail cry out for evaluation. But *every* contact with individuals or groups of givers is worthy of careful evaluation.

What went well? What did not? If the program clearly went too long, how are you going to adjust the program of the next event? If the individual you met with expressed a deep concern about your organization, how are you going to address that concern, and when? If you sent out a mail appeal for funds, what was the result and how did it compare with the cost? Were there any complaints? How did response to this letter compare with response to previous letters?

Effective organizations evaluate everything on a regular basis. Evaluation is not occasional; it is part of the rhythm of organizational life.

It requires the humble acknowledgment that every interaction with stakeholders in your organization is important and, no matter how successful, can be improved. Your message can be clearer. Your follow-up can be better. Your gift acknowledgments can be more prompt. Your publications can be sharper. Your meetings with constituents can be more regular and focused. Settling for "good enough" is a recipe for mediocrity. Careful, consistent reflection marks successful programs and appropriately serves those who partner with you in accomplishing your mission.

Grow their base.

If you can count 1,000 or 100,000 individuals who are engaged enough with you to be a current giver, be sure of this: that number is in flux, either growing or contracting. You must never take for granted something as precious and precarious as thoughtful, generous engagement of individuals in the life of your organization. The best organizations are intentional about growing their base of support.

> THE BEST ORGANIZATIONS ARE INTENTIONAL ABOUT GROWING THEIR BASE OF SUPPORT.

Those who don't are exposing themselves to the natural inertia of unfulfilling relationships. Growing your base involves keeping those who care for you and winning new friends. Here are ways you can grow your base:

Keep your promise. Inherent in every mission, every organization, every church is a promise. We declare why we exist. We define who we serve. These are the outcomes of our activities. These are the returns on investment givers can expect. The most reliable way to keep your current givers and win new ones is to consistently keep the promises you have made, both implicitly and explicitly. If we cease to reflect our mission or lag in visible outcomes, we do not deserve the support of God's people. The responsibility to keep the promise of your organization goes well beyond the work of any development effort. It is primarily in the hands of the CEO and the board. If they are attentive to these matters, the organization will be. If they are not, it will be evident to all.

Keep telling your story. If you are confident that your organization is keeping its explicit and implicit promises of performance, then you are free to tell that story. Publications, websites, events, and individual meetings are all powerful ways to keep those who are investing in you and to win new stakeholders in your cause. Institutions tend to be quick to dismiss those who have drifted away from us in their interest and support. It is easy to rationalize that "They just don't get it" or "They are not true givers." While it is certainly possible that a giver's animating passion can shift away from our mission to others, it is probably more accurate to assume that if a donor has drifted away, it is because we have not fulfilled our responsibility in that relationship. In our busyness, we may have taken their support for granted. Perhaps we were careless in saying thank you. Maybe we neglected to stand alongside them in a period of personal or financial need. Or maybe we just assumed that they knew our mission well and did not need us to keep telling them why we exist or what the fruits of our efforts have been. Often when *we* think we have adequately communicated, we have not communicated enough. To grow your base, keep telling your story—and tell it well.

> OFTEN WHEN *WE* THINK WE HAVE ADEQUATELY COMMUNICATED, WE HAVE NOT COMMUNICATED ENOUGH.

Ask for involvement. Did I mention that asking for involvement is important to getting in the kingdom? Thoughtful stewards, no matter what their capabilities, have limited time, energy, and resources. Often the tipping point to involvement is the simple act of asking. "Would you lend us your expertise in this particular area?" "Would you take this survey to help us better understand those who support us?" "Would you give to this particular project?" Dynamic organizations who take their givers and potential givers seriously will provide varied and meaningful ways for people to become engaged with them. They will *ask* for that engagement. And they will grow their base. Strong programs require intentionality, discipline, and creativity, and the result is more satisfying for the giver and the organization. It also most certainly honors the One in whose kingdom we serve.

CHAPTER

THREE GIFT TYPES, AND WHY YOUR ORGANIZATION NEEDS ALL THREE

The wisdom of the wise is an uncommon degree of common sense.
—Dean Inge

He is gentle and wise. He served one institution his whole career. He was spectacularly successful at attracting major gifts but would deflect any credit for it. Most who gave as a result of his efforts would call him a friend before they called him a fundraiser. In short, David Dunlop is my hero in the work of getting. So when he shared his insights on three kinds of gifts and the dynamics that surround them, I paid attention. And, fortunately for you, I secured his permission to share his rubric of the three gift types. All three gift types are already present in the group of men and women who currently give to your organization. Every well-rounded program meticulously cultivates regular, special, and ultimate gifts.

REGULAR GIFTS
Regular gifts are the most common gift to any institution. They usually come in response to the giver's question, "What should I give today or this month or this year?" A regular gift is often given in

response to a general ask, like a direct mail appeal, an email blast to a large group of potential givers, or a phonathon call. Because appeals to regular gifts are often related to annual operational needs, they are timed to the institutional calendar more than the timing of the giver. These gifts also tend to be on the smaller end of what givers typically can and do give—although the "smaller" gifts that some are able to give are five and six-figure gifts. Regular giving requires little to no personal cultivation of relationship. It is transactional in nature: asking, receiving, and thanking—and asking again.

SPECIAL GIFTS

Special gifts are often given by people who are already making regular gifts to the organization. They differ from regular gifts in that they arise from a particular and more individual request from an organization for a particular purpose. A gift given in response to a capital campaign or a particular effort to pay off a mortgage at a church are examples of a special gift. The gifts are requested and received in relation to the timing and needs of the *organization*. They are typically five to twenty times larger than regular gifts. Because these gifts involve more personal asks, relationship is part of the equation. But because the timing and needs of the organization are the motivating factors, this type of gift still has a transactional quality.

ULTIMATE GIFTS

Ultimate gifts are of a different nature altogether. They represent the giver's full capacity to give, whether it is the janitor bequeathing his $150,000 estate to the hospital he served or Warren Buffet's $26 billion gift to the Gates Foundation. These gifts can be five hundred to one thousand times larger than any previous gifts. But they do not only differ in amount. The timing is determined by the *giver*, not the institution. Because of its size, an ultimate gift is often, though certainly not always, given by bequest after death or in the form of a trust or other planned gift instrument. With ultimate gifts, an ask is seldom necessary or appropriate. Ultimate gifts grow out of the heart of the giver and his or her relationship (often lifelong) to the institution. Givers of ultimate gifts are usually well beyond the need to be asked.

INCORPORATING ALL THREE IN YOUR PROGRAM

Most nonprofits (there are 1,514,530 of them in the United States) operate almost exclusively at the level of regular gifts. In one sense, this is understandable. The need to meet operational budgets loom largest for most nonprofits. Also, limitations of budget and personnel make broader, less personal appeals most cost-effective—at least on the surface. And, frankly, it is easier to make broad, general requests than to develop relationships that can generate special and ultimate gifts. But to stay in the realm of regular gifts is poor stewardship on the part of *any* organization and underserves the true giver.

Nearly every "regular" giver is capable of giving a special gift periodically. If your organization is stuck in the mode of regular, transactional giving, you must carve out institutional resources to build relationships and conceive special opportunities (e.g., campaigns, special projects, innovative programs, etc.) for special gifts. It *is* time intensive and broadens gift horizons from monthly or annually to multiyear, but that investment will pay huge dividends as givers respond to deeper involvement in the life of the institution.

While nearly every regular giver is capable of special gifts, there are a few of your special givers with the financial capacity and potential to give an ultimate gift that can transform your organization. Undoubtedly, several givers that you already know possess the resources and potential passion to give the gift of their fullest capacity to your organization. Every giver, at any level, is worthy of our best effort. But intentionality with the handful of high-capacity givers in your orbit represents a great opportunity to advance your organization's work in the kingdom. Developing ultimate givers rarely happens apart from intentional effort.

How do you grow the regular giver into a special giver and a handful of them into ultimate givers? First, engage every giver and potential giver as carefully and thoughtfully as you can. Seize every opportunity to draw people closer to the heart of your cause. Be an organization that exudes transparency and authenticity. Listen well. Ask appropriately. Keep your promises. And ask God regularly to lead gifted givers to you for the sake of His kingdom.

Think of your list of regular givers. Is it 100? Or 100,000? Regardless, there are at least a few on your list of regular givers who have the capacity and latent desire to give your organization a special gift that could be multiples of the actual gift they gave this year. And somewhere on that list is at least a handful, maybe many more, with the capability—at a time of their choosing—to give your church or organization a gift that could transform your ability to accomplish your mission. Don't limit yourself by thinking one or two dimensionally. All three kinds of gifts should be regular parts of advancing your mission. With intentionality and the work that meaningful relationships require, you can be God's instrument to help unleash the full capacity and generosity of many in service to the kingdom.

11

GETTING THE WORD OUT

Homer: "Oh, what am I gonna call my Internet company?
All the good names are taken."
Marge: "What exactly is it your company does again?"
Homer: "This industry moves so fast it's really hard to tell."
—The Simpsons

NOT SELF-PROMOTION BUT SELF-DISCLOSURE

If any word conjures more cynicism and disrespect than *fundraising*, it may be *marketing*. Unfortunately, many readers of this book are responsible for the bad associations with both! How does a believer, operating in and for the kingdom, engage in marketing—or should you at all? How does modesty, humility, and honesty fit with the imperative to persuade people to support your organization?

My greatest insight into the true nature of marketing came under the counsel of a whirlwind of a consultant, Patti Crane of Crane MetaMarketing, Ltd. Patti is a fountain of ideas that challenge static thinking. A number of years ago, we were engaged in the process of homing in on just what differentiated the mission and purpose of our organization from similar institutions. As often happens when a group of thoughtful Christians discuss this topic, someone asked, "Should we even be talking about how to promote ourselves to the public? Isn't it God's job to defend us? Can't we just be who we are and leave the results up to Him?"

There was a long pause as we shared knowing looks around the room. It was obvious that many shared that sentiment. Then Patti spoke, carefully and deliberately. "I can see where some would find the whole matter of self-promotion unbecoming of an organization committed to expanding Christ's kingdom. But, people, we are not talking about self-promotion here. We are talking about self-*disclosure*."

The whole point of marketing came clear to me on that cold March morning, and it made perfect sense to every person in that room. We weren't creating ideas to prove we were better than others whose ultimate purpose was the same as ours—advancing Christ's kingdom. Our responsibility was to accurately *disclose* who we are and where we fit in the work we were called to do. This simple but powerful truth can free up any organization to do the very important work of disclosing its reason for being and presenting to the public a cogent rationale for support. Once we come to terms with marketing as it should be in the kingdom—self-disclosure, not self-promotion—we are free to think creatively about the many ways available to us to present who we are and why we exist. Maybe marketing, even in the kingdom, makes sense after all.

> ONCE WE COME TO TERMS WITH MARKETING AS IT SHOULD BE IN THE KINGDOM...WE ARE FREE TO THINK CREATIVELY ABOUT THE MANY WAYS AVAILABLE TO US TO PRESENT WHO WE ARE AND WHY WE EXIST.

PUBLICATIONS STILL COUNT

In an age when nearly everyone is connected electronically, with a dizzying array of options to obtain and deliver information, printed publications still count. There is something about the tactile nature of a magazine or newsletter and its nearly anachronistic delivery through the mail, of all things, that holds strong appeal to givers and other friends of your organization. A recent survey from a sophisticated marketing/development operation—one with websites, online communities, direct mail, and phoning programs—revealed that 71 percent of constituents reported, surprisingly, that their primary source of information about the organization was from the institutional magazine. Moreover, this percentage was quite consistent across generations. Of course, the importance of a regular print publication to its supporters will differ from organization to organization, but advancement efforts must be careful not to abandon this proven means of communication. What does a publication provide that a website or online community cannot?

Stability.

How your organization is perceived is important. A paper publication, depicting the people and programs of the organization, evokes confidence that the organization lives, breathes, and thinks. Even campaign brochures serve the purpose of conveying the organization's thought, commitment, and stability. The real work of engaging people in a campaign is best done in person with, perhaps, a simple "white paper" in hand. But to leave behind a thoughtful brochure that demonstrates careful planning and commitment to the numbers and the goal of the project can reassure stakeholders that the campaign is an integrated, well-planned effort. Publications evoke stability and planning in a way that other media do not.

Durability.

Over the years, I have been in many homes to talk with givers and potential givers. I have yet to see a computer screen open to the website of my organization! But I regularly see a magazine or commemorative book from my organization somewhere in sight. There is durability to printed materials that cannot be duplicated by more ethereal channels such as websites, social media sites, and email correspondence.

Touch.

There is a reason I read the *New York Times* electronically during the week. But one of my little luxuries is reading the *Times* in its print version on the weekend. The electronic version is convenient and time efficient. The paper version provides more leisure, more time, and more enjoyment. I suspect the same is true for many givers to our organizations. A publication can easily be put in hand and interacted with in a satisfying, in-depth way—and not just at one sitting. It can be easily referenced multiple times over an extended period of time. Never underestimate the value of publications to touch and be touched by those with whom you care to maintain an ongoing relationship and conversation.

> YOUR WEBSITE PROVIDES EASY ACCESSIBILITY, THE ABILITY TO MEASURE TRAFFIC, ALL IN A CHANGEABLE AND INTERACTIVE FORMAT.

YOUR WEBSITE IS A LIFELINE

While print communication is a key component to disclosing the uniqueness of your organization, the Internet has become a new and powerful medium for communicating with and listening to our stakeholders. One nonprofit organization recently discovered that the equivalent of 30 percent of their constituency visits their website every *month*! That should get the attention of every organization concerned with keeping and winning friends. Your website provides easy accessibility, the ability to measure traffic, all in a changeable and interactive format.

Instant accessibility.

What was unthinkable a generation ago is now upon us. We have the ability to convey nearly unlimited information about our mission, our organization, our people, and our programs to anyone at any time! It is an opportunity that no organization should ignore or enter into lightly. Just as a publication needs an editorial focus and voice, so does your website. If nothing never happens (chapter 7), the instant accessibility of your website is a powerful tool that must be carefully planned, updated, and measured.

Measurability.

Most means of communication are difficult to measure. How many recipients have opened and read your magazine or your direct mail? It is difficult to tell. But it is easy to know how many people are accessing your website and even what sections of your website they are looking at (and, of course, what sections they are ignoring!). This adds weight to the time and resources we give to creating and maintaining the website, but also helps us focus our resources on information that is meaningful to stakeholders.

Changeability.

Once an article is written or a brochure is printed, it is in its final format—ready or not! But the web is different. It can be updated hourly, if need be. A picture of the recently retired president will endure on the annual report for a year, but it can be changed on the website the day the new president arrives. Of course, changeability is only an asset if the organization has allocated enough resources to take advantage of the opportunity. If you don't dedicate enough time and care to keep up-to-date, your audience will know it, and you may compromise your credibility.

Interactivity.

Another benefit of any website is its potential for interactivity. Some websites are built for the dissemination of information alone. But fully utilizing the tool for the benefit of its users means providing opportunity for users to respond. An article about an emergency need in a remote region served by the organization can include a link to a giving site so givers may not only be made aware but can respond with questions, encouragement, or financial support. It can take three or four months for a reader's response to an article by the CEO to appear in the "letters to the editor" department of a print publication. By contrast, a reader can respond instantly to the same article on the organization website, and the CEO can follow up within days. This interactivity must be managed, of course, but it allows the organization to respond to a greater number of stakeholders.

There are other applications of the Internet that present opportunity and peril to any organization, namely, social networking sites.

NETWORKING

Social networking, through such media as Facebook, LinkedIn, and Twitter, is an emerging force that will profoundly affect most nonprofit organizations. Whether or not we are prepared for it, social media will have an increased role in how we relate to all sectors of our constituency, and, more important, how they relate to (and about) us. If the Pope is tweeting, we should at least consider the form of this medium.

Until recently, even in the Internet era, electronic communication has remained largely under the control of the organization. Even websites with instant interconnectivity are a relative static medium, where the messages are created and managed by the authoring organization. Social sites, by contrast, drive and shape the conversation and message.

Consider the relief agency monitoring its own activity in a crisis center somewhere in the world. They send email messages out to their list of people who want to be informed of this activity. They post regular updates on their website, including video clips from the caregivers in the region. These are helpful and accurate, but controlled messages. But there is also a relief worker on the ground with her own social networking site, providing valuable information with her worldwide circle of friends and supporters, largely beyond the reach and control of the organization. The worker's network might even provide an inlet for humanitarian aid that is outside the scope and control of the sponsoring organization.

What has happened? Control (a valued commodity for any organization) has a viable work-around that may not necessarily work at counterpurposes to the organization, but neither is it necessarily in concert with the organization. On the upside, the autonomy and power of an independent networking site might generate more information and more aid than any one organization could. On the downside, it might also generate confusion on the part of the constituency and even work at cross-purposes with the relief agency.

Here's another example. A Christian university is ramping up an online program to help its seniors and recent alumni access other alumni for vocational guidance and networking. An email hits the in-box of the alumni director, thanking the school for the wonderful service they were able to access through LinkedIn. The service bore the name of the university and was all about vocational networking. The only problem? It was not created by the university; it was created by a thoughtful, enterprising alumna who saw a need and took it upon herself to provide this service to her fellow alumni. There is nothing inherently wrong or right about this. The reality is it is beyond any organization's ability to stop or change. While this example represents someone of goodwill providing a valuable service to their alma mater, the same technology can be used by someone of ill will who is (justly or not) critical of some aspect of the organization's activity.

The issue, then, is not control or management. It is recognizing the democratization of the power to shape opinion about your organization. Beyond being *aware* of this new and powerful communication tool, there are at least two things an organization can do to deal with it.

First, listen well. Being aware of groups who are having conversations about your organization can teach you a lot. What is it about your organization that warrants a conversation? What stirs passion among those who care about your mission? What are they paying attention to? What are they agreeing and disagreeing with? What is accurate and what is bogus? What deserves a reply, and what is better left unchallenged? Listening is not spying. It is an act of kindness toward a group of people who care enough to engage in conversation about you. It takes more time and discernment than has ever been required of a nonprofit organization. But it can also be a window into how your organization and its programs are perceived.

Second, the organization can appropriately engage conversation via social media. We must keep in mind that social discourse on the Internet may be less civil than more traditional communication. Nonetheless, the wise organization will have a sense of the "groundswell" on the Internet, and choose carefully when and how to respond. But far more important than responsiveness is proactivity. Rather than seeing social media as a threat, the savvy organization will embrace its potential on its own terms by engaging those who use this medium.

Should a church have its own Facebook site? Should the senior pastor be active on Twitter? The better question might be, "Do we have a credible reason *not* to engage significant segments of our constituency through these media?" One strong warning: the quickest way to lose credibility with this important and growing audience is to establish a site without the institutional will or resources to maintain it. Engage social media carefully, but don't neglect this resource as a wonderful opportunity to get the word out—to accurately and faithfully disclose who you are and your place of service in the kingdom.

THE POWER OF EVENTS

Bringing givers and potential givers together with key people in your organization will never go out of style. It can be a dinner for a thousand friends of your organization or an intimate meal hosted by the CEO for several friends. It can be a golf outing with a 144 golfers or a fishing trip with the president and chairman of the board and a dozen friends. It can be a two-week travel experience with a group to see firsthand the work your organization does or a quiet meal at a halfway house with a handful of men transitioning from prison to a new life. Events of any kind are key moments to engage people in your mission. Why? Any giver or potential giver who agrees to engage with your organization through an event has told you, merely by their presence, that they have interest in an ongoing and even deeper relationship. Done well, events can accelerate and deepen relationships for a lifetime. Done poorly, they can do damage to one of the most important possessions of any organization—reputation and relationships. If you do not have a regular program of varied, excellent events, you have overlooked a principle way to engage and grow your givers.

Here are a few essential elements of an events program that will enhance spreading the word about your organization.

1. Variety.

People are different. Some have time and a desire for extended interaction. They are perfect candidates for an immersion weekend or even an extended trip related to your organization. Many others have demanding schedules that require much deliberation on whether or not to expend the time for an event. They may be better candidates for a dinner engagement. Some love to travel and think little about getting on a plane to interact with organizations they care deeply about. Others, because of time or circumstances, rarely choose to travel or to commit more than a few hours. They require the organization to plan an event close to them. Some love intimate conversation with only a few. Others are more comfortable with the distance and relative anonymity of a larger event. Adapting the nature, location, and length of events is a tangible way any organization can demonstrate care for givers. Falling into a pattern of one mode of event for all will certainly exclude many who would engage in other types of events. Creative, varied events mark the sophisticated development effort.

2. *Quality.*

Quality does not mean expensive. Quality means care for details and for guests who have given their time to deepen their relationship with you. One of the most meaningful events I have ever attended was a lunch of black beans and rice at a small ministry that meets prisoners at the prison gate upon their release and ushers them into an intensive, fifteen-month program of mentoring, discipling, and preparation for life after prison. I was invited by the head of this national ministry, a gregarious Cuban, an ex-offender himself, to visit the house where five former offenders were living in community. The house, while simple, was immaculate. The men were disciplined and courteous. We ate a simple but lovely lunch during which each man shared his story. I was captivated by the simplicity and the power of what was taking place less than a mile from my comfortable office. There was nothing opulent, but the quality was impeccable.

The level of engagement and degrees of comfort in interacting naturally differs across your constituency. Events can and should vary greatly in size, location, and purpose. Still, it is not so much the venue but the quality of the planning and the care for the individuals that will be memorable. And this will often be rewarded with a willingness to consider deeper involvement in the life of your organization.

3. People-centered rather than money-centered.

The great temptation, once people have agreed to attend your event and hear (or rehear) your story, is to focus on giving and need. But even a casual consideration of the needs and desires of the attendees will reveal their desire to reacquaint themselves with your mission and your people. What is new and noteworthy in your work? What are your successes and challenges? How are people benefitting from your programs? What do you need to expand your service to people?

We've said it before, but it bears repeating: people hate needs, but they are attracted to vision. Tell a compelling story. Highlight the opportunities. Reveal your challenges. True givers will often respond positively. And if, when you ask them to carefully consider their involvement,

> IF WE GENUINELY TAKE CARE OF PEOPLE IN OUR EVENTS, THE RESULTS WILL CARE FOR THEMSELVES.

they thoughtfully decline, you have done your part, they have done theirs, and the rest is in the hands of God. If we genuinely take care of people in our events, the results will care for themselves.

4. Review and adapt.

The very best events can be better—always. Evaluate. What went well? What was missing? Where did you miss your audience with less than compelling content? Sometimes these are hard questions. But review and revision are part of the care that getting in the kingdom requires. Celebrate your successes. But review and adapt—every time.

BEING WHO YOU ARE

What does it mean to be engaged in disclosing rather than selling your organization? Fundamentally, it requires an uncommon level of transparency. Anyone with enough interest in us to give from their personal resources *knows* we have shortcomings. We don't need to lead with our failures and shortcomings, but neither should we pretend they do not exist. To be sure, this is easier to accomplish through one-on-one dialogue than through a public medium, such as a website or institutional magazine. But transparency should shine through our active communications too. Sometimes it can take the form of self-deprecating humor, showing that we do not take ourselves too seriously. Or it might take the form of a description of a program that is not up to our own standards and expectations, accompanied by an explanation of what we are going to do about it. It might be an article about someone who has benefitted from the work of your organization and who, because of circumstances, would never be a poster child of your greatest success but is nevertheless an encouraging example of God's activity in a broken situation.

> AUTHENTICITY IS WINSOME TO GIVERS WHOSE OWN LIVES ARE MARKED BY STRENGTHS AND SHORTCOMINGS.

Organizations that experience successes *and* failures and disclose them both appropriately convey a ring of authenticity. Organizations that tout only their brilliance and successes do not. Authenticity is winsome to givers whose own lives are marked by both strengths and shortcomings. Be who you are, even while making known your aspirations and successes. This is "marketing" at its best and is worthy of service in the kingdom.

CHAPTER 12

THE **CAPITAL CAMPAIGN**

History does not repeat itself, but it often rhymes.
—Mark Twain

It is difficult to find a nonprofit group that has not conducted or considered a capital campaign. There is a "must-have" quality to the idea of a capital campaign. Presidents love the idea. So do board members. And why not? Campaigns characteristically provide laser focus on the mission and aspirations of the organization. Their use has stood the test of time; they have been around for many generations. For the organization, a campaign is a compelling reason to ask, and for the donor it's a compelling reason to give. Campaigns often engender much larger commitments from individuals and even foundations than most year-in and year-out efforts (see chapter 10). Done right, the capital campaign draws together the champions of the organization to accomplish what could not have been done in a "business as usual" mode. It also helps win new champions at higher levels of involvement and financial support. And, of course, campaigns tend to make news: "University Kicks Off Billion-Dollar Campaign" or "Local Hospital Adds Cardiac Care Unit with Record Gift to Campaign." What's not to like!

In truth, the capital campaign can be a significant milestone in the life of any nonprofit organization and should be carefully considered as an appropriate vehicle for advancing the organization's mission. Even so, there is a time for such an effort, and there are circumstances that make a campaign ill-advised. There may even come a time in its life when the organization moves beyond campaigns (see chapter 13). To understand the power of the capital campaign, we must carefully define its elements, offer clues for determining whether an organization is ready for such an effort, and examine factors that can lead an organization to new levels of donor involvement and support.

WHAT IS A CAPITAL CAMPAIGN?
Capital campaigns can vary greatly in time frame, size, and content, but there are elements common to all. The capital campaign is a coordinated effort, rooted in planning and the essential mission of the organization, to secure extraordinary gifts and pledges over a specified period of time for the highest priorities of the organization.

THE ELEMENTS OF A SUCCESSFUL CAMPAIGN
Planning.
Campaigns are not to be entered into lightly. Because successful campaigns are so dramatic in their impact, some organizations launch them to accelerate results rather than to fulfill careful planning. But the best campaigns are rooted in a thorough planning process. And *institutional* planning must precede *campaign* planning. A capital campaign is not a pretext for getting more money! It is a natural outcome of planning and vision that involves all the key stakeholders in the organization.

Even the smallest nonprofit can be a complicated enterprise with many competing values and interests. There are typically many constituencies: the board, the administration, the staff, givers large and small, and, of course, potential givers who share your mission with their interests or passions. Each one has a vested interest in the organization, although each has a different level of accountability and knowledge.

As with any healthy enterprise, campaign planning must begin with the executive leadership interacting closely with the board of directors. It is these groups of women and men who must understand and embrace the unique mission of the organization. Planning bereft of mission and focus is merely assembling a wish list with the hope that potential investors will fulfill your wishes. But an organization whose leaders are crystal clear on its reason for being and its unique call to action is in a strong position to actualize its mission. That is why the CEO must lead the board in understanding the organization's particular place in the general landscape of the enterprise. For example, providing subsidized or free legal assistance to those who otherwise could not afford it is *worthy*. Providing subsidized or free legal assistance to immigrant families on the west side of Chicago to help establish healthy, functioning communities is *powerful*. Being a Christian university is *laudable*. Being a Christian university that is highly selective of well-balanced Christian young people to engage the world as whole and effective Christians in every conceivable vocation is *compelling*. Being a church in your community is *obedience* to the Lord of the church. Adapting the timeless purpose of the church to the unique needs of your community can be *transformational*.

Long before building projects, endowments, or program enhancements (the *what*) comes clarity on the *why*. Why do we exist? How would this world or the kingdom suffer if we did not? What do we do best? And—this is important—what are we involved in that saps our resources and strengths but is not integral to our mission? This list might include good and worthy endeavors, but good planning is not just about adding; it may involve strategic subtraction to reallocate resources to the core purposes of the organization. After all, organizations are as responsible for their own stewardship as are the individuals and foundations that support them. And an organization that clearly uses its resources well raises the confidence of potential investors.

Case for support.

Specific planning begins with clarity of mission and purpose. Again, this must begin with the CEO and board. If current resources, properly accounted for and allocated, are not adequate to advance the mission of the organization, then the organization must envision projects, programs, or resources that will do so. That is when the leadership of the organization can initiate the planning of a capital campaign.

Whether adding physical space, strengthening the operational budget, endowing a program, or all of the above, the leadership is free to dream and to put dreams to paper. What might a new facility look like and cost? What would an increased gift income stream enable the organization to do? What would full endowment of a new program mean for the future viability of the ministry?

These are all important questions for establishing the case for others to support the vision of the organization. The dreaming and planning can now be committed to writing and, more important, submitted to other key stakeholders.

Feasibility.

Of course the mission, dreams, and specific plans will remain unfulfilled without key partners to fund the vision. Partners get to vote twice on the dreams of the organization—once in the planning process and again with their financial investment! The feasibility study is the important step of taking the first vote: does the institution's mission and strategic plan match the passion and purpose of the thoughtful steward?

I had the pleasure of consulting with a well-established Christian ministry that had a dynamic, visionary president. He had asked me to meet with him and his development team and to spend a day with his board of directors. They had big plans for several high profile building additions. They were wondering about the process of organizing a campaign effort. As I began talking about mission, values, strategic planning, and the case for support, the president proudly handed me a lovely four-color brochure outlining the two building projects with beautiful architectural rendering of each project. Apparently the president and his board had decided what was best for the organization and were now going to go to their constituency to find out if they were in or out! I had to gently tell them that perhaps they had gotten the cart before the horse. While the leadership of the organization had done *its* planning, they had left many of their key stakeholders out of the deliberation process.

> PARTNERS GET TO VOTE TWICE ON THE DREAMS OF THE ORGANIZATION—ONCE IN THE PLANNING PROCESS AND AGAIN WITH THEIR FINANCIAL INVESTMENT!

The feasibility study is best conducted in a white paper format. Four-color brochures can come later. A white paper is a thoughtful reflection on the vision and projects that have emerged from the planning process to date. A white paper communicates, "Here is our best thinking and planning about our future direction and funding priorities. What do you think? What do you like? What do you have questions about? Do you agree that this represents a high priority moving forward? And, if you agree with these priorities, are you willing to support us financially to accomplish this? If so, what range of gift might be possible?"

There are at least two ways to think about the time-consuming process of soliciting donor feedback before launching a capital campaign. Some see it as dangerous to involve key stakeholders in this way. What if you discover that those whom you were certain would love your project think it is either a bad idea or not a high priority? What if they offer a completely different priority or approach than you had considered? They might reveal a much lower capacity or willingness to give than the organization was counting on. Dealing with these surprises could put you behind your timetable or even render your existing plan difficult or impossible to implement.

But there is another way to view the process of a feasibility study, and that is to embrace it as an important tool for measuring and honing your own planning document. The organization should welcome questions and comments, even challenging ones, as a means to test the planning that has already been done and, more important, to involve the stakeholder in the planning process. In general, the more comments and red markups your potential investor puts on your white paper, the better.

> THE END RESULT OF LISTENING WELL IS THE CONCEPTION OF A STRONG PARTNERSHIP.

Why? It indicates care and a willingness to participate in the outcome! It may cost time and effort to interact with new ideas. It will surely require tact in responding to ideas that don't conform to the missional goals of the organization. But the willingness to listen, interact, respond, and revise appropriately clearly demonstrates that the organization wants to partner with, not dictate to, the donor.

The end result of listening well is the conception of a strong partnership. Mutual participation ensures that the donor's vision is not co-opted by the organization nor the organization's mission co-opted by any individual or group. The eventual solicitation is not transactional—"Are you in or out and at how much?"—but relational —"How can we accomplish our common vision together?" And the board has a wonderful tool, the results of fifteen to one hundred or more substantial conversations (depending on the size of your constituency) with key stakeholders, from which to make its final decision on the size, scope, timing, and content (in other words, "feasibility") of the project. That is the power of a thoughtful, thorough feasibility study as the preface to a capital campaign.

Movement and direction are critical.

The CEO and the board have reaffirmed the organization's mission, evaluated current use of resources, and presented a plan that requires participation from stakeholders. They've tested these plans with those who know and care most for the organization: its staff, key donors and volunteers, and potential donors. Not only have they tested, they have truly listened. The revised case for support demonstrates it. The size of the goal, the time frame to achieve the goal, and the specific campaign components are clearly articulated in the revised case for support. Now what? Movement and direction are critical.

Inside to out.

Before an organization looks outside its domain for support of a capital campaign, it must look inside. Once again, this begins with the board. It is one thing for a board to say to its president and development team, "We approve of you going out to get as much money as possible!" It is quite another to assume responsibility both for the initial commitments to the new campaign and for its final outcome, as well.

I was at a meeting where the board was deliberating approval of the start of a campaign. We had discussed the specific projects, their costs, the results of the feasibility study, and had gauged the readiness of the president and his team to carry forward this proposed five-year effort. When the time came for the vote, the chairman of the board made a startling and bold challenge to everyone in the room. He looked around the table, paused, and then said in a sober, deliberate tone, "Ladies and gentlemen, we are embarking on a program that will require a lot of our president and his team. But I don't want anyone around this table to vote yes unless you are committing with your giving, your advocacy, and your time, to do not whatever you can but whatever you *must* to ensure the success of this effort."

The room fell silent, and for good reason. The chairman was calling the trustees to their ultimate responsibility for the institution. As trustees, they did not have the luxury of cheering from the sidelines or giving what was comfortable. They were charged at the onset to do their best throughout the entire campaign, all the way to its successful conclusion. As you might imagine, most of the financial and volunteer commitments were sacrificial. The board led not only with their vote but with their firm commitment to the success of the effort. Consequently, their leadership strengthened the hand of the advancement team throughout the campaign.

Campaigns must start from the inside and move out. But the concentric circle of involvement and commitment is not yet ready to move beyond the organization. Next comes the organization's employees.

You might be thinking, You're not suggesting that the administration and staff of the organization should, in addition to their stellar service and often less than competitive salaries, be asked to give to the campaign effort? That is what I'm suggesting. And I believe this is integral to the success of the campaign. Here's why.

The first and primary reason relates to my assertion at the beginning of this book: God created us to give and imparts a joy in that giving that surpasses human understanding. The story is told of a fund drive in a church setting. A number of people came forward to give significant gifts. Among them was a woman who was nearly destitute. The pastor, wanting to spare this dear woman, said, "Thank you, but you put that money back in your purse. You need it to care for your family." Her response rebuked a temporal view of giving. She said, "Pastor, please don't rob me of the joy of giving what I am able to give." There are many in our organizations who serve, yes, to provide for their families, but also because their hearts have been captured by the mission. It would be wrong to pass them over. In fact, it would rob them of joyful participation.

There will, of course, be others in the organization who are less mature in their thinking about giving. At its worst, it manifests itself as, "How dare you ask me for money! I am making less than I could make in the private sector already, and I give most of my time and energy here as well." Some organizations refuse to ask for financial and other kinds of campaign commitments from staff members to avoid this kind of backlash.

Should every employee of every organization give on a regular basis? To the kingdom, yes. To the organization itself? That is a matter of spiritual discernment and decision, but I would question giving your vocational life to an organization that you do not deem worthy of your financial support.

My counsel is to press ahead. Do it gently, but do not neglect the gifted and thoughtful donors among you in deference to the less mature givers. Instead, use it as a teaching opportunity. Encourage the gifted givers among you to tell their stories. It will rekindle nearly everyone's deeper reasons for serving with your organization in the first place. It might move some to reevaluate the eternal truth that "where your treasure is, there will your heart be also." It will certainly energize giving once the campaign moves out to the broader constituency. When you are able to report that a significant portion of your staff has committed some measure of financial support and time, it reinforces that your campaign is about funding what is integral to the mission of the organization.

At this point, the board is fully invested in the capital campaign. The administration and staff who were involved in the planning and in funding the priorities are on board and invested as well. It is time to move from the center of your organization to your broader constituency. But the order is important.

Up to down.

We have already seen (chapter 5) that money is not distributed evenly, nor does it come in that way to any organization. *Every* gift is important, but the reality is a small percentage of the gifts to any campaign lend disproportional financial support to the success of the project. Therefore, resist the temptation to go to anyone and everyone next. Your most financially capable friends who already embrace your mission are the ones you need to approach first for financial commitment to your campaign effort. The larger (up) gifts must precede your smaller (down) gifts. Always remember that every gift to the kingdom is precious in God's sight, so each one must be precious in ours as well. But in this world the variation in wealth and interest in our little part of the kingdom requires us to be wise in our approach.

> EVERY GIFT IS IMPORTANT, BUT THE REALITY IS A SMALL PERCENTAGE OF THE GIFTS TO ANY CAMPAIGN LEND DISPROPORTIONAL FINANCIAL SUPPORT TO THE SUCCESS OF THE PROJECT.

That reality brings us to a time-honored tool: the gift table. Whether your project costs $100,000 or $100,000,000, the gift table keeps an organization from kidding itself about the possibility of fulfilling its vision. Gift tables are far from infallible. God can bring resources to any enterprise in whatever manner He chooses, but He often rewards the organization that plans prudently. And, generally speaking, without the handful of top-level gifts, there will never be enough individual gifts at the lower levels to achieve the total goal.

The elements of a table of required gifts is illustrated here:

$100,000 Project

Qualified Potential Donors	Potential Donors Needed	Gifts Needed	Gift Amount	Projected Total At This Amount	Cumulative Total
5	5	1	$10,000	$10,000	$10,000
10	6	2	5,000	10,000	20,000
20	12	6	2,500	15,000	35,000
35	25	15	1,000	15,000	50,000
40	35	20	600	12,000	62,000
40	35	20	500	10,000	72,000
100	75	50	250	12,500	84,500
300	100	many	>250	15,500	100,000

A gift table should roughly track the following proportions: The lead gift for any effort should be at least 10 percent of the total campaign goal. The next 10 percent should come from two or three individuals. The top twenty-five to fifty gifts (or so) should comprise up to 50 percent of your total. The next one hundred or so individuals should bring you close to 75 percent of your goal. The remaining (and important!) 25 percent of the goal will come from all the rest, whether "all the rest" is two hundred or twenty thousand givers. These ratios hold true in an amazing number of campaigns, almost regardless of the dollar goal or the number of potential givers.

As you lay out a possible scenario for "gifts needed," it is important to have a sense of the number of donors you are aware of who may have the capacity and propensity to give a gift at the level you require. As you can see from the illustrated gift table, it is prudent to have more potential investors than gifts you expect at any particular level. Look at the $10,000 gift level above. It would be ideal to have five potential donors you could talk with about this lead gift amount. Why do you need more than one qualified potential giver if you need only one gift at that level? Because there is so much we don't know before we converse with potential givers. One person, though financially capable, may be dissatisfied with us to the extent that a lead gift is out of the question. Another may reveal that we have been mistaken about their financial capability. Another couple may be capable of giving such a gift, but their level of involvement with us and care for our mission does not rise to the level of a lead gift of $10,000. That leaves, perhaps, two givers with the capacity and propensity to give the level of gift you feel you need to achieve your final goal. We must not make hasty assumptions about any individual's ability and willingness to give.

Individuals and institutions are human, and consequently have some capacity for self-deception. This is revealed in statements like, "The money's out there," or, "I'm sure Alice will come through with the lead gift," or, "Rather than presuming on our own planning and strategy, let's just trust God for the outcome." Being wise about how money tends to come in for projects is a strong platform from which to see God's unique work in your mission through the lives of thoughtful Christian stewards. The prudent organization conducts its campaign from up to down.

Quiet to public.

There is another time-honored principle of conducting a capital campaign that is worth heeding and discussing: moving from a quiet to a public phase. To announce to the world any campaign before planning, testing its feasibility, and asking key stakeholders about their intentions to participate is foolhardy. That $250 million goal may be wildly unrealistic, given the paucity of planning or the readiness of key friends. It is also possible that the $250 million goal has wildly underestimated the capacity and willingness of the constituency to support your mission. In the former case, you may damage the organization's reputation by failing to attain the goal. In the latter, the leaders may be guilty of poor institutional stewardship by selling short the organization's potential for a major move forward. Either mistake may cause you to diminish what is precious to possess and difficult to recover: a fine reputation.

Both situations can be avoided by not rushing to announce to the world what you are planning. In the course of a campaign, there will be plenty of time for that. Do not grow impatient with the deliberate, quiet planning and engagement of your board and key stakeholders. It will pay off in confidence and momentum when you are ready to announce to all what has been accomplished, and what is yet to come.

Knowledge to involvement.

Institutions value knowledge. Thus we're tempted to think, *If only people knew our need, our opportunities, our mission, they would surely give.* But while institutions value knowledge, *people* value involvement. Thoughtful Christian stewards do not only have resources to give; they also have insight, experience, and a deep desire to give their hearts and passions, as well. The challenge, then, for every nonprofit organization is to transform stakeholders from distant observers to integrated partners in its mission. Brochures inform and videos may inspire, but partnership *involves* people in the mission. The single greatest shortcoming of campaigns is relying on presenting information as a substitute for involvement. Sending a wish list to potential donors is a poor substitute for engaging them in a dialogue about the desired results of a particular initiative.

Of course people want information: What is the project? What will it cost? What kinds of gifts are necessary for it to succeed? How can I make a difference? But what distinguishes the adequate from the excellent campaign is materials, events, and interactions that call people to action. The best campaigns change people from passive, informed observers to active participants in the work of the organization.

TELLING THE STORY

Every successful campaign presents a compelling narrative. The institutional mission is clearly stated and carefully linked to the objectives of the campaign. The narrative avoids the language of "needs" and accentuates opportunities. It is short on what is in it for the organization and long on the benefits of participation. Fundraisers are forever asking people to fulfill institutional goals, when what people deeply desire is to fulfill institutional *mission*.

If it is true that dollars chase ideas but never catch up with needs (and it is!), then we must create a narrative that clearly points to the certain result of collaboration. An endowed position in the organization will relieve the budget in perpetuity, but enabling more resources to be applied to the mission is what the donor cares about. Achieving the annual fund goal is important, but adequately providing for every aspect of the organization is compelling. A fully funded building will enhance the bottom line of the organization, but it is the people who will be served that energizes significant gifts.

Telling the story well is a major function of the capital campaign. You can't spend too much time telling your story succinctly, movingly, and clearly. People generally support only what they understand and find compelling. Tell your story well, and you will enable thoughtful stewards to envision what can be accomplished with their investment.

FLUIDITY WITHIN STRUCTURE

The nuts and bolts of day-to-day campaign management are beyond the scope of this book, but a general operating principle is in order.

The course of a campaign—typically three to five years, although it can be longer—is clearly a marathon, not a sprint. Done correctly, it reflects careful planning and the most strategic priorities to secure the future of the organization. But three to five years is a long time, and many things can change during that span of time. This calls for a campaign structure that is firm but also flexible.

We've already stated that donors/investors get to vote on our projects twice—once in the planning stage and again in the funding stage. As long as the organization has its eyes firmly on the mission of the institution, midcourse adjustments are permissible. For example, let's suppose a relief organization has, as part of its campaign plan, the establishment of a staging center for its activities in Kuala Lumpur. It has been researched carefully, built into the campaign plan, and is clearly a strategic advance. However, circumstances on the ground prohibit the original location and a new location opens up in Manila. Does Manila need to wait until the next campaign? Not at all. There needs to be flexibility to go back to those who have supported the original project (Kuala Lumpur), explain the circumstances, and ask permission to reallocate their resources to the new site. Change within the structure and priorities of an organization should not be worrisome or problematic if organizations keep moving ahead in partnership with their donor/investors. A reasonable level of adjustment should be expected in any long-term funding effort.

CELEBRATION

A successful campaign is no small effort. And there are no small campaigns. If planning has been thorough and visionary, the goal will be a challenging one, whether it is $10,000 or $100,000,000. A successful campaign is also no small accomplishment. It typically represents well over a year of intense planning, followed by three to five years of promotion, events, conversations, exhilarating highs and deflating lows. In the process, don't forget to celebrate accomplishments: successful events, milestones (such as reaching the halfway point), closing that all-important lead gift, and, of course, reaching the financial goal of the campaign. In your celebration, include not only the major gifts team but also the unsung heroes who set up the appointments,

> PEOPLE GENERALLY SUPPORT ONLY WHAT THEY UNDERSTAND AND FIND COMPELLING.

receipted the gifts, and otherwise contributed to the effort. Make sure to acknowledge the CEO and the board as well. And, by all means, find ways to thank and celebrate with donors at special dedications or other celebrations. As in other venues of life, offering simple, heartfelt appreciation is the right thing to do and is a grace that often returns in abundance to the giver. It is also a corporate opportunity to give thanks to the Giver of all good gifts, God Himself.

REFLECTION

Fundraisers, and for that matter boards and CEOs, tend to be doers who often need to be more intentional about taking the time to reflect. But to complete a major campaign effort without reflecting upon what went well and what can be learned for the future is a strategic mistake. Reaching the goal is not the only mark of success. Were the events and solicitations mission-centered and people-centered, or were too many of them merely transactional? Did you deepen relationships with donors? Did you expend your campaign costs effectively? Did you say "thank you" well? Are detailed plans in place to continue to report to donors on the value their gift is bringing to the organization—not just when the gift is given or when the campaign is complete but for many years to come? How can you do even better next time around? Taking care to evaluate and learn for the future is part of what distinguishes good efforts from great ones. It also differentiates principled, Christ-honoring, people-centered getting from mere fundraising to meet a goal. Reflection is its own reward and befits the principled fundraiser.

INNOVATIONS

The basic elements of the capital campaign we have discussed have stood the test of time. But without innovation, the campaign can become formulaic rather than a dynamic expression of an organization's highest goals. The following list of possible innovations will assist in making your campaign all it can be:

Social media.

In past years, it was innovative to create a campaign-specific website that could be accessed by anyone who wished to find out about the progress of the campaign in general or an initiative of the campaign in particular. In the age of social media, that innovation lacks "stickiness," that dimension that draws people back. Forming groups that have a stake in the week-to-week progress of a campaign—successes, challenges, curves in the road, and testimonials by givers—can provide the interest and momentum needed to sustain a multiyear effort. How about a blog by the CEO or periodic updates from the pastor discussing what is being learned about giving, getting, and God's people? How about "tales from the front" that chronicle significant encounters with individuals or particularly meaningful events? Social media provides the means to tell stories and, perhaps more important, to really listen to those who truly care about the outcomes of our funding efforts.

Comprehensive vs. project.

Campaigns can and should take on different forms that fit the objectives of the effort and the culture of the organization. A key consideration is whether to tie all giving (operational, planned, and capital) into one goal (comprehensive), or to single out a particular project (the renovation of the church sanctuary) while separately appealing for the operational and missions budget. Campaigns seem to be gravitating to the comprehensive approach, primarily because every gift during the campaign period can be a contribution to the "big" campaign effort. It helps everyone to feel a part of the success of a large, combined effort and gives more flexibility for the organization to apply unrestricted gifts to areas of greatest need.

Length.

Another decision to be made is the length of the campaign. There are at least two considerations. First, how long will it take to appropriately challenge and receive commitments from every eligible stakeholder? Sometimes, eighteen months is plenty of time. For larger organizations with national constituencies, it may require closer to five years.

The second consideration is the pledge fulfillment period. Often the size of gifts needed for success of the campaign requires extending the fulfillment period. If an individual can give $100,000 in year one, it is reasonable to assume that a five-year fulfillment period would enable a commitment of $500,000 or more.

Other considerations on the proposed length of the campaign include: size of the financial goal in relation to past giving, stability of the donor base (a national university will have greater opportunity for a longer campaign than, say, a local church, where membership and affiliation is more transient), past experience, and the current vibrancy of the economic environment.

Visual storytelling.

Telling your story over several years and many geographical regions almost certainly requires a video version of the case for support. But be careful. The temptation is to prepare a "moving picture" version of the printed case statement with charts, goals, and appeals for funds. There are two predominant trends in video presentations. One is to shorten them to ten to twelve minutes. If a video is longer than that, no matter how scintillating we believe the content to be, we will lose most of our audience. The other trend is to steer away from need and point instead toward outcomes. A beautiful rendering of a completed building is stirring on one level. A picture of what it can mean to the development of people who will use the building is moving and powerful.

Events.

We have already discussed the nature of events in the course of a campaign. People are busier than ever. If prospective givers will travel to your location and spend a weekend being immersed in your mission and potential for the future, great, but there will be others who have only an evening to give, or perhaps a scant hour in their offices. The trend is to prepare long and short versions of your story that convey essential information and meet the time requirements of those willing to hear the story. With events, one size does not fit all.

Endorsements.

Credibility is important in engaging people in your campaign. Some organizations, because of many years of performance, already have credibility. Other newer or lesser-known organizations seek endorsements of highly respected individuals, who can lend their credibility to their lesser-known missions. Celebrity is not necessarily important, but a person of substance and reputation can bolster the case for support of your mission.

Capital campaigns will endure because they focus the attention of the organization on what is mission-centered. They also provide the thoughtful, engaged giver with a compelling reason to help advance the organization in a dramatic way. But, like any endeavor, vision, planning, and careful execution elevates a mere program to greater service in the kingdom.

CHAPTER

BEYOND CAMPAIGNS

*It's easy to come up with new ideas; the hard part is letting go of
what worked for you two years ago, but will soon be out of date.*
—Roger von Oech

Everything that can be invented has been invented.
—Charles H. Duell, Director of U.S. Patent Office 1899

The joy is in creating, not maintaining.
—Vince Lombardi

Campaigns can be powerful. They focus the institution and its
constituencies on its mission. They often far exceed previous
giving totals and nearly always provide visible signs of progress, such
as new buildings, new personnel, or new programs. The achievements
of successful campaigns are a legitimate source of institutional pride
and provide momentum and new benchmarks from which to launch
future efforts. It may, therefore, take courage to even think about
moving away from campaigns to something different. But in this
chapter, we will do just that. We will look at a few potential pitfalls
of traditional campaigns and ways to move beyond them to an even
more effective way of winning friends and support.

HOW CAMPAIGNS CAN FALL SHORT

While the benefits of campaigns are evident, there are ways in which they are hard on any institution. Campaigns operate on the level of focused need, requiring immediate and sometimes heroic action by givers. They demand much of key stakeholders, the advancement team, and the CEO. It is not uncommon for campaigns to end leaving pastors or presidents, advancement staff, and even givers with some degree of burnout. Besides the toll campaigns take on gatherers and givers alike is the reality that campaigns tend to focus more on the institution's needs and timetables than that of the givers. Is there a way to move beyond traditional capital campaigns to a more organic approach to funding major institutional priorities?

IS THERE A BETTER WAY?

Many elements of campaigns should continue, particularly the meticulous planning required to identify institutional needs, align them with mission and current resources, and engage donors to come alongside in realizing the careful planning. But rather than a rigid time frame of a campaign (usually three to five years), a cycle of planning, execution, and more planning can become the rhythm of an organization—one in which givers can become involved, not necessarily on the institution's timetable but within a careful collaboration between capable and willing givers and a thoughtful, forward-looking institution.

It might not require abandoning the structure of a campaign so much as letting the structure (time frame, gifts required, fancy names, and big finales) fade into the background and allowing the ongoing conversations about the organization's future and direction come to the fore. Here is what it might look like.

Your organization is well established. You have been around a long time—fifty years or more. The public knows what you are about and has a favorable view of your value to the kingdom and/or society. You have a relatively stable group of men and women who regularly and generously lend their support of time, wisdom, and financial resources. Your president embraces the fundraising task and is comfortable engaging your organization in a continual and dynamic planning process. Your board has the vision to fund a development team that is seasoned and productive. You have probably completed several successful capital campaigns in recent years, each one larger than the last. In fact, you may have conducted one campaign after another with little or no pause in between.

If this describes your organization, you may have an opportunity to move beyond campaigns. Instead of talking with your principle givers about institutional goals once every five years or so, maybe you can engage them in an ongoing conversation about adequately funding operational and aspirational goals. It is a conversation not just about what you need now but about how you envision the future—ten, even fifty years out. What pieces need to be in place so you can move to new levels of service and influence? What can you begin now that can bridge you to that better place? What can you learn that will enable better decisions in the future? And, perhaps most important, where and *when* can the true giver make the most of their giving to you?

There may be a time to move back to a more traditional, time-bound, goal-bound campaign. And it would be irresponsible to cede planning and decision making beyond the administration and board. But wouldn't it be refreshing, particularly to givers, to engage in an in-depth conversation about the future of the organization they love and care for? To have conversations about ultimate gifts (chapter 10) when it makes the most sense for the giver? To really listen to the hopes and dreams of donors/investors for the organization? To be willing to adjust plans and timetables based on givers' readiness to become involved? This way of operation probably takes *more* planning and vigilance than a traditional campaign! But it might have the effect of more deeply involving people in the life of your organization. And with that involvement can come levels of engagement and gifts that would exceed what any organization could do with a traditional campaign. There may come a time, in the process of giving and getting, that is just right to move beyond campaigns.

CHAPTER

14

THE UNIQUE **CHALLENGE** OF **FUNDRAISING** IN THE **CHURCH**

The local church is the hope of the world, and its future rests primarily in the hands of its leaders.
—Bill Hybels

WHY SO DIFFICULT?

Any treatment of asking God's people for God's money for God's work that does not consider the unique challenges of funding the ministry of the local church would be inadequate. After all, the church is God's primary means of doing His work in the kingdom. If money fuels ministry in Christian endeavors outside the church, it surely fuels ministry within the church. And, of course, all the dynamics of giving and getting exist in the church: theological understanding, generosity, centrality of mission, and call to action.

But the church is different from any other cause or organization. It is a community of like-minded people who voluntarily assemble as a group on a weekly basis. That in itself is a distinctive trait. The level of intimacy and involvement is unlike that of any other organization. There is spiritual (pastoral) leadership to which the congregation has willingly submitted itself and that speaks about the mission to the whole community every week. There is a governing board vested with not only fiduciary authority but spiritual authority as well. There is a great variety of size, polity, worship style, and organization, all guided by a common "handbook" of operation, the Bible.

Because the local congregation is called by God to extend His kingdom in its sphere of influence, gathering resources for the mission of the church is not optional. The only question is whether or not it is done well and in keeping with the direction of the Lord of the church, Jesus Christ.

THE ROLE OF THE PASTOR

Although some pastors may resist it, they have the primary responsibility as shepherds of God's flock to shape attitudes and actions related to giving. No one has to remind a pastor of the God-given responsibility to equip the congregation with the "whole counsel of God." And, of course, the intimate relationship between a person's possessions and soul is a central theme of the biblical record, particularly the teachings of Jesus Himself. Also, no one in the congregation knows better than the pastor that money and possessions are a point of tension in families and church budgets alike!

What, then, are the obstacles to taking clear pastoral leadership in the matter of funding the ministry and outreach of a local church?

The pastor's personal practice.

Some pastors, like many others, haven't had the privilege of growing up in a home where careful management of finances and generous giving was modeled. Unfortunately, some pastors themselves have fallen into the same debt trap as some of their parishioners. It is difficult to lead in a matter as fundamental as stewardship when your own practice reflects failure or disobedience.

Lack of training.

Another culprit can be seminary education itself. There are many pastors who went through years of seminary training with nary a word of counsel about equipping the congregation to be rich toward God! Many enter the pastorate ill equipped to lead in the intricate matter of managing the resources entrusted to the church by its members. It is amazing that a subject so fundamental to the success of the local church is so often overlooked during pastoral training. But even if a pastor goes through seminary and into the church without a biblical and worldly-wise understanding of money, wealth, and giving, there are many resources available to equip the leadership of your congregation in this important area. Form a group of gifted givers and mature believers from within your congregation and ask them to mentor you in the principles of kingdom giving and ways you can lead your congregation. Or seek out a Christian firm with deep experience in this area, such as Generous Church (http://www.generouschurch.com). The best pastors never stop growing in their understanding of spiritual truth that can strengthen their congregations for service in the kingdom. What could be more important than leading your flock in understanding and applying God's standard for giving in the kingdom?

Perceived attitudes in the congregation.

By its very nature, a congregation is made up of a cross section of society with different perspectives and levels of maturity in the matter of possessions, money, and giving, and of course, differing financial capacity. Ask the financial secretary in any church, and you will learn that the same dynamics we observe in the mind of donors (chapter 4) appear in the church pew. There are gifted givers, thoughtful givers, casual givers, and even nongivers. We would like to believe that Christian behavior in the matter of giving and personal stewardship

> "IN THE MATTER OF GIVING IN THE CHURCH, THERE ARE USUALLY FOUR GROUPS OF PEOPLE IN EVERY CONGREGATION: THE UNABLE, THE UNWILLING, THE UNINFORMED, AND THE UNINSPIRED."

is markedly different from society at large, but sadly, it is not.

A consultant to local churches in the matter of giving, whom I greatly admire, has said that "in the matter of giving in the church, there are usually four groups of people in every congregation: the Unable, the Unwilling, the Uninformed, and the Uninspired." Unfortunately, too many pastors cater to the notion of those who are "unable"—a safe and pastoral-feeling stance—instead of preaching to the unwilling, the uninformed, and the uninspired! A pastor cowed by immature attitudes about giving, such as "My money is my business" or "I can't afford to give" or "Why are they always asking for money?" will never be able to lead the congregation into generous, joyful giving.

Failure to preach "the whole counsel of God."

For some of the reasons stated above, it is easy for a pastoral team to avoid the topic of money and possessions and reserve teaching, preaching, and counsel on this topic for the (dreaded) "stewardship Sunday." There is no stronger argument for preaching through whole passages or books of the Bible when teaching in the matter of stewardship. Periodic preaching on matters of stewardship when there is a particular financial need feeds the notion that money and giving is either a peripheral issue or an uncomfortable topic to be addressed only when absolutely necessary! However, God's ownership of all we possess, His overwhelming gift of grace (see chapter 1), and our eternal debt of gratitude are central themes of the biblical text. Teaching Christ-honoring stewardship should not be "gotcha" moments in the life of the church but central concerns of life in the kingdom that are addressed through the full preaching ministry of the church.

It is nearly impossible for a governing board or a congregation to rise to the biblical standard for money and possessions without strong pastoral modeling and exhortation. The good news is that many pastors are willingly taking up that challenge. Those who do will lead their flock to greater service in the kingdom and their church to greater relevance in the community.

THE ROLE OF THE BOARD

The church holds high standards for its leadership—and well it should. The early church set the bar: "Be shepherds of God's flock that is under your care, serving as overseers—not because you must, but because you are willing, as God wants you to be; not greedy for money, but eager to serve, not lording it over those entrusted to you, but being examples to the flock" (1 Peter 5:1–3). Here's how the governing board of the local church can foster a healthy, generous church community:

Encourage and empower the pastoral staff.

Equipping the pastoral team in the matter of stewardship is a fundamental responsibility of the governing board. Perhaps all that is needed is encouragement and even permission to challenge God's people to be rich toward God in using all their gifts of time, talent, and treasure. You might bring in competent counsel (see chapter 15) or send your staff to training opportunities offered by such organizations as Generous Church. If pastors sense encouragement, leadership, and expectations from the boards to whom they report, they will more intentionally and joyfully fulfill their duty to "see that [their congregations] excel in the grace of giving" (2 Corinthians 8:7).

Evaluate giving trends and health of the congregation.

Part of the spiritual and fiduciary oversight of the congregation is measuring its financial health. Without violating the confidentiality of individual givers, boards can assess not only giving *totals* but giving *trends* as well. Too many churches simply measure giving totals. If giving this year is better than last year, it is easy to conclude that all is well. But giving totals might mask the more important issue of whether individual members of the congregation are growing in their understanding and practice of becoming joyful and generous givers. If the numbers indicate the congregation is not growing in this important area, then there may well be a failure of leadership to affect the growth of individual giving. Through surveys and discreet reports from the financial secretary, year over year reports can measure number of givers, frequency of gifts, largest gifts by an individual, increases or decreases in giving from family units, and the number of members and regular attendees who give nothing at all. It is only by being aware of what direction and with what intensity generosity is moving in your congregation that the leadership can begin to measure its effectiveness in helping those gifted in generosity to apply their gifts while calling all God's people to become obedient and joyful givers in the kingdom.

Lead by example.

Leading by teaching and encouragement is important, but leading by example is powerful. The governing board of the church should not fear scrutiny of their commitment to living generous lives in the church. I was at a predominantly African-American church during its Sunday morning worship service. I don't know how common this is, but it made a powerful impression on me. The pastor was leading worship from the pulpit. His wife was sitting on the platform. While other announcements were being made, the pastor's wife opened her purse and pulled out her checkbook and a pen. She carefully wrote out a check, tore it from the check pad, and kept it in her hand until the offering was taken. She then very deliberately stood up, walked over to the usher, and placed the check in the offering plate. My first reaction to this was a bit uncharitable: "She's telling the whole congregation, rather immodestly, that she and her husband give regularly to their church." But I've thought about it many times since. What she was really doing was teaching the whole congregation by example. Her actions spoke more eloquently than any pastor's words could: "It is right and good to give to God's work through our church."

I'm not suggesting that the leaders of the church sit on the platform every Sunday and write checks in front of the congregation (but I'm not suggesting they don't, either!). But sharing stories of how God has grown you as a steward is a way to lead the congregation by example. In any special effort, it is right and good for the congregation to know that every one of the governing board has made a commitment to the effort commensurate with their ability. Sharing anonymous stories of generous gifts received (regardless of the amount, of course) is another way to contribute to the growth of the congregation in the grace of giving. Testimonies of specific journeys of generosity by givers in the congregation can be powerful examples and motivators to generous stewardship.

> LEADING BY TEACHING AND ENCOURAGEMENT IS IMPORTANT, BUT LEADING BY EXAMPLE IS POWERFUL.

THE ROLE OF THE CONGREGATION

The congregation of a church consists of a group of men and women who have voluntarily gathered to worship God and to receive instruction and encouragement to live their lives in conformity to God's holy will. It is a pity, then, that so many churches declare God's will for salvation, personal holiness, and love for their neighbor, but ignore an issue that touches every member every day—money. It is hard to imagine that anyone in any congregation would be content to be unable, unwilling, uninformed, or uninspired! The pastors and leaders must be willing to convey the whole counsel of God, even about money. I suspect that most members who care enough to submit themselves to the discipline and instruction of the church would be receptive to hearing the plain teaching of Scripture on money, possessions, and eternity. The church that is open and honest about the place of money in the life of the kingdom has the best chance to overcome the inertia of a nonkingdom perspective on giving.

HOW TO TALK ABOUT MONEY IN THE CHURCH
In the daily life of the congregation.

Some churches excel naturally and positively in calling their congregations to generosity, but many do not. Here is a checklist of healthy attitudes and actions in the life of the church that can transform the discussion of money and stewardship from awkward and apologetic to a natural component of being a faithful follower of Christ:

Confront the pretext of "unable to give."

By and large, the notion that an American is unable to give is preposterous. To be sure, there is a large spectrum of available resources to give in service to the kingdom. The "widow's mite" (Mark 12:41–43) is compelling evidence not only that even the very poor have *something* to give but that such a gift is precious to God, far out of proportion to its monetary value. Too often, however, it is deemed godly and pastoral to offer a "pass" if someone feels too financially strapped to give. Behind protestations that one is unable to give may lurk many a self-centered spirit or a series of bad choices that make it difficult to release *any* resources.

Challenge those who are unwilling to give.

As delicate as it is to confront a selfish spirit, what could be more anathema to a follower of Christ than a self-centered orientation in a desperately needy world? Some of the other ways to talk about money in the church, listed below, are natural and easy ways to teach and challenge the "unwilling" to think biblically about the matter of giving. It is a pastoral duty to do so.

Teach those who are uninformed about giving.

My sense is that most who do not give are not selfish people. They have simply not been taught or shown the joy and meaning attached to the act of giving. They grew up in a home where giving was not modeled or the weight of living in a consumer-driven economy had snuffed out the ability and will to give. But such a person did not identify with your congregation for no reason. There is some level of willingness, maybe even desperation, to live in greater conformity to an eternal kingdom than a temporal one. The wise pastoral team will seize opportunities to teach the joy and responsibility of joyful giving.

Motivate those who are uninspired to give.

Failure to give may not be motivated by a selfish spirit at all. The church may simply have failed to offer compelling reasons to give. People generally give only to causes they understand. Are you clear about what the operational budget of your church enables in terms of outreach and ministry? The pastoral and leadership teams may be totally convinced that an addition to the educational wing of the church will transform opportunities to nurture the whole church family, but if they have not winsomely conveyed that to the congregation, who is at fault—the givers or the leaders of the church?

Sermons and special campaigns are not the only times to motivate and educate the congregation in the grace of giving. Every worship service, especially at the time of the offering of gifts, is an opportunity to teach and inspire. Unfortunately, the words are often the same—something like, "We give because all that we have belongs to God." This is true, of course, but there are so many other reasons the follower of Christ should give, and pastors need to take every appropriate opportunity to teach and inspire. Beyond *ownership*, we can talk about *commitment*. We commit to *generosity* to help demonstrate that God, not money, comes first in our lives. We should give out of *gratefulness* for God's abundant grace extended to us. We give out of *obedience* to God's Word. We give with *trust* in God alone for His provision to us and His use of our resources in His service. We give with *joy* because our gifts will benefit others and encourage them in the grace of giving. We give with *compassion*, because it reflects God's compassion. We give with *freedom*, because our hope rests not in earthly things that will soon pass away but in the eternal. Take every opportunity to motivate God's people to live and act counterculturally in the use of their resources. Many will respond to bold, clear proclamation of these truths.

Share examples of people who have exercised the gift of giving.
There are at least two rich sources in teaching generosity that can be sprinkled throughout the life and conversation of the church. One source is Holy Scripture. There are scores of examples of generous, joyful giving in Scripture, but I will name just a few: the building of the tabernacle in the time of Moses (Exodus 36:6–7), the believers at Antioch (Acts 11:27ff), Barnabas (Acts 4:36ff), the Corinthian believers (1 Corinthians 16:3; 2 Corinthians 8:10), the Jerusalem believers (Acts 2:44ff; 4:32ff), the Macedonian believers (Romans 15:25ff; 2 Corinthians 8:1ff), and the Philippian believers (Philippians 4:10ff). All were challenged by leaders to give (aided, of course, by the work of the Holy Spirit) and the result was provision for the work of God and the joy of His people.

The second resource for teaching generous giving is your congregation. Make opportunity for gifted givers in your congregation to share their journey of generosity. It will capture the imaginations of others and could be just the teaching moment to move people to action.

A woman in a local congregation had made a commitment of $5

per week to a building project at the church. After several months the pastor asked her to share with the entire congregation the amazing ways God had affirmed her faith and provided, often in miraculous ways, the resources she needed to fulfill her commitment. The impact on the congregation was palpable. Ask people to tell stories. How did they discover the joy that comes from giving? How has it changed their life? Far from a point of pride or self-promotion, these gifted givers can be used by God to encourage many others in their thinking and practice of giving.

Ask.

Here we return to a central theme of this book. If it is good and right to call God's people to lives of obedience to their Creator, does not the use of monetary resources fall within that call? If the operational budget of the church is bearing fruit in the kingdom, should God's people not be asked to participate? If giving is a tangible way to assert that this earth is not our home and that God is the owner of all we have, is it not a spiritual service to ask God's people to make that declaration? In reality, the manner in which believers use all the gifts God has given is important to the Lord of the church. Asking God's people to give may be just what God uses to unleash the gift of giving. We fall short of the transformational power of the gospel by not preaching and living the whole counsel of God. Generosity of spirit and faithful stewardship of all that has been entrusted to us is central, not peripheral, for the true follower of Christ. If you are a pastor, live and preach it unapologetically. And when the time comes, do not hesitate to call God's people to generous, joyful giving.

Pray.

Calling God's people to be generous in spirit goes beyond the realm of teaching or persuasion. It quickly crosses over into the spiritual dimension that calls upon God's people to pray. To encourage giving in the church is an opportunity to enlist the gifted prayers in your congregation to exercise that gift. They can pray for the leadership of the church in contemplating and formulating bold plans for the future of the congregation. They can pray for open hearts to be moved by the opportunity to give. They can pray for the pastor(s) who will encourage the flock to be generous. They can also pray for God's intervention as stewardship decisions are being made. Praying earnestly in the realm of giving reinforces that, while the leadership of the church "plants and waters" in the whole matter of giving, it is God who "gives the increase" (1 Corinthians 3:6).

> ASKING GOD'S PEOPLE TO GIVE MAY BE JUST WHAT GOD USES TO UNLEASH THE GIFT OF GIVING.

When the time calls for an accelerated giving period.

It is as true for the church as for any organization that relies on individual stewardship to fund its mission: there are times in the life of the church when being true to its calling requires an accelerated giving period. It might be to fund a new building or a major addition/renovation. It might be the planting of another church. It might be the retirement of a mortgage to free funds for other ministry opportunities. It might be for a new program of outreach and service that the congregation is called to pursue.

Many of the elements of the capital campaign (chapter 12) apply. But there are nuances that are unique to the church setting. Following is a sequence of events that can be followed not only to achieve needed funding for a particular project but to nurture God's people as faithful givers in His kingdom.

Secure clarity on the project to be pursued.

While it seems self-evident that consensus in any voluntary organization is a necessary first step in funding any special project, it is easy for a pastoral team and board to move faster than the congregation is prepared to move. After all, they have been appointed to provide leadership and they have the closest vantage point to see opportunities for ministry expansion. But many grand and promising visions—and pastors—have been abandoned because they failed to bring God's flock along with them. The time and patience required to present the project and its underlying vision to all the stakeholders is critically important to its ultimate success. Clear plans and cost projections are imperative. It is essential that the pastor and leadership team cast the vision over a period of months. Small group opportunities to interact with the vision and the project are time-consuming, to be sure, but they can overcome a multitude of future objections and second-guessing. One-on-one meetings with influencers in the congregation (past board members and longtime members) can yield consensus and wise direction in the planning process. Achieving clarity on the project to be pursued and the ministry-related reasons for moving forward is the first essential step in preparing the church for a period of accelerated giving.

Determine resources needed to succeed.

Counting the cost of a specific project is a natural stewardship requirement of any church leadership team. It begins with the dollar cost, but involves much more.

Dollars.

Getting the financial costs of any project right from the beginning is essential in building confidence throughout the congregation. There is nothing more discouraging than stretching to secure a goal and finding that the target has moved, not because of unpredictable factors like the economic conditions of the region but because of lack of thoroughness when counting the cost. Expending money at the beginning to seek outside verification of the entire financial and congregational impact of the anticipated project easily pays for itself in the later stages of an accelerated giving season. This is also the time to create a gift chart that indicates the number and size of gifts you will need to achieve your goal (see chapter 12). Of course, God can (and will) provide the needed resources in His way and in His timing. But the prudent will observe how money tends to flow in any such effort.

Staff.

Another part of counting the cost is to be realistic about the impact the effort and resulting new program or building will have on the budget and other church resources. Are there enough personnel or dependable volunteers to promote the effort? Are the key pastoral staff willing to persevere for the duration of the project? Change in leadership midstream can devastate a major funding effort.

Time.

Have all the time factors been considered? How much time will it take to conceive a careful plan for the new program or facility? How long do you think it will take to build consensus in the congregation? How about the time it will take to challenge and solicit financial commitments? How long will it take for commitments to be fulfilled? While campaigns in the nonprofit sector can anticipate pledge fulfillment periods of five or more years, the nature of church life and attendance probably requires a much shorter period of two to three years. You must anticipate cash flow and the time value of money. With careful planning, time can be your best friend. On the other hand, moving forward without a reasonable time frame can spell discouragement and even failure.

Consultants?

Some churches have a built-in aversion to seeking outside counsel. For one thing, it is expensive. For another, it feels a little bit like a lack of faith. Hasn't God equipped the church for such a thing as a season of accelerated giving? By all means, look first at the resources within your congregation to help the leadership thoroughly think through this important period in the life of the church. But there is no shame in looking to outside counsel from firms and individuals that have worked through similar projects scores of times. The time that can be saved may justify the cost. Moreover, the unknown opportunities such professionals can identify may make outside counsel indispensable to success. The leadership team should interview several individuals or firms and check references thoroughly. And the team should reach consensus that the individual or firm suits the tenor of the congregation.

CAREFULLY REVIEW GIVING HISTORY

It is essential to know and evaluate certain giving and stewardship teaching data before embarking on an accelerated season of giving. The following list is adapted with permission from the elements of a "Generosity Audit" used by Generis, a very capable consulting firm on church giving and generosity:

1. Weekly giving history from at least the past twenty-four months. This will provide a baseline from which to project the potential for a larger effort.

2. History of past campaigns in the life of the church. What were the goals? What actual funds were committed? What actual funds were received? How many family giving units gave and what were the amounts? (These figures do not need to identify the families.)

3. Number of first-time givers per month over a twenty-four-month period. Many churches do not track this, but it provides a picture of potential. A similar report of those who have ceased to give in a twenty-four-month period (usually due to moving away from the church) can help you anticipate potential decline of givers.

4. An assessment of teaching and preaching on stewardship in

the past two years. Has there been systematic challenge and teaching in the church community or is there a deficit to be made up? A congregation that has been led well in the joy and obligations of giving is in a much better place to embark on a period of increased giving than a congregation in which money is essentially a taboo subject.

5. An analysis of how your staff is organized and how well equipped they are for this kind of churchwide effort. Deficits of personnel or expertise should be addressed and factored into the cost of the anticipated project.

6. Membership and attendance statistics for the past twenty-four months. What are the trends and how do they correlate with actual giving?

7. The financial balance sheet for the church and the last two full annual budgets and actual receipts. Such an audit is time-consuming and detailed. But careful analysis can prevent the leadership of the church from under- or overanticipating the congregation's potential to fund a major new project. Does this kind of detailed planning lack faith? Hardly. Any funding project that will stretch the congregation in their giving and vision requires a lot of faith—regardless of meticulous planning!

Reaffirm pastoral and board commitment to the project.

Once all of the planning and analysis is complete, it is prudent to review the plan, both for the project and for securing the funding of the project, with the board leadership and staff. If you have done your work, the congregation's enthusiasm and commitment will sustain you as you bring the whole congregation along to achieve your God-given goals. Part of the reaffirmation process is securing financial commitments from the board leadership and the entire staff. Commitments need to be commensurate with capability and the priority of this project in the minds of the leaders of the congregation. To do all the prep work well but then fail to lead with your giving will discourage the congregation and likely will lead to falling far short of the church's potential.

Seek commitments from key stakeholders.

We have already seen that money does not flow evenly, inside or outside the church (chapter 5). In any congregation, a few individuals with accumulated assets will provide 20 to 50 percent of the total needed for your project (chapter 12). Frankly, their gifts are not more important in God's sight. You can count on the fact that some of the smaller commitments to the project will be given more sacrificially than some of the larger ones. Nevertheless, you should first secure commitments from those who have shown by their previous giving that they have larger capacity (hence the generosity audit). You also need to include in this group those who, by their vocation or other indications, may well have the capacity to make leadership-level commitments.

Once you have identified these people, how do you make contact and seek commitments from them? First, the group might represent 20 percent of the family giving units in your congregation. Most will be people with higher capacity for giving, but do not neglect to include some other key opinion makers and longtime, godly members whose commitment will be crucial to the effort. Gather smaller groups of these stakeholders (perhaps ten to twelve couples at a time) for an evening meal and discussion with the senior pastor, key staff members, and representatives of the governing board of the church. This is an opportunity to restate the vision and project. It is also the time to share the reality that gifts from a few in the congregation will create the capital and momentum for all of the congregation to participate (the gift table can be a powerful tool to demonstrate this reality). Then, rather than telling each one to go home, pray about their commitment, and eventually turn in their commitment card, ask only one thing of them—their willingness to have an individual meeting with the senior pastor and perhaps one other board member to talk through their commitment to the project. While some churches and pastors balk at this suggestion, it is essential and appropriate for the spiritual leader of the church to have a conversation with a family in their parish about the very spiritual matter of stewardship of personal resources. Is an ask involved? Probably, but if the vision has been cast well, the ask will be a natural part of the conversation. Is it an occasion to talk someone out of money they do not have or intend to give? Of course not. That would run counter to the true nature of giving. A pastor who has thought through Christian stewardship, taught it well to the congregation, and modeled it should have no hesitation in asking God's people for God's money for God's purposes in the church. This may not be easy. But the pastor is called upon to do many things that are not easy or particularly comfortable for the sake of God's work.

Tell stories.

Once the pastoral staff, church leadership, and a concentration of other key stakeholders have made their commitments, there will be a number of stories to share with the congregation at large: How skepticism about the project was transformed into enthusiasm. How the opportunities made possible by the project moved an individual from having a closed hand on their resources to having an open hand. How adopting God's view of wealth and eternity enabled a couple to look not only to their income but also to their assets in fulfilling their joyful obligation to the project. As the congregation sees the commitment of the leadership and the resources that have already been committed, they can begin to see the possibilities for the success of the project and the ways their personal stewardship can be used by God to grow them as givers in the kingdom.

Challenge all.

At this point, feel free to ask the entire congregation to commit to the project. It is probably not possible to have individual conversations with every member and regular attender of the church. However, it is wise to give every member of the congregation an opportunity to request a meeting with a senior member of the pastoral team to discuss their questions about the project as it relates to their personal giving. But larger informational meetings (patterned after the small dinners with key stakeholders), followed by distribution of commitment forms or instructions on how and when to indicate participation, can be a successful vehicle to involve everyone. There may be natural affinity groups for these types of gatherings such as new members, already established small groups, etc.

Utilize technology.

Churches are increasingly utilizing technology in creative ways in worship and church life. Technology can also be employed creatively in keeping the purpose and themes of the accelerated season of giving before the congregation. Video can be a powerful medium to connect people to a particular project. Social media can engage a whole segment of the congregation that wouldn't think of filling out a pledge card or wouldn't know how to fulfill a commitment with a check! Online giving opportunities, a staple in the nonprofit world, can be used effectively in the church. Websites and social media can keep a large segment of the congregation up-to-date on progress, challenges, and the status of their own commitments. Giving kiosks in the church can facilitate regular updates and opportunities to make and update pledges. Using technology well is not clever or gimmicky. It is part of the responsibility of church leadership to engage congregants in ways that are familiar and intuitive to large swaths of the congregation. They must also use care not to remove the act of giving from the context of worship, where it clearly belongs.

Tell more stories.

As you are gathering and tallying commitments, you will hear more stories about releasing resources for eternal purposes that can be shared with the congregation. This might be the time for a culminating, all-church banquet or special gathering to announce the results of the total effort.

"Firstfruits" offering.

Soon after reaching the goal, it is important for the church to conduct a "firstfruits" offering. This is essentially the gathering of the first "payments" on the multiyear commitments that have been made. This is important for two reasons. It builds momentum (and capital) early in the payment season, helping to secure the promised total. Second, some builders and/or banks that are fronting some of the needed capital in anticipation of the cash payments may require an early payment to justify their investment. Additionally, offerings to God's work represent gratitude to God, who has poured out His grace through the Lord Jesus Christ. The firstfruits offering is a wonderful opportunity for worship and celebration of corporate obedience to building Christ's kingdom through His church.

Say thank you to God and His people.

Showing gratitude is not only the right thing to do, it is the natural response to God's work within a church family. The pastor can provide ample opportunity for the congregation to give thanks to God: for the resources He has made available to the congregation, for moving His people to give in a way that reflects His ownership of all their resources, etc. And showing gratitude to each individual giver is important too. Pastors and leaders can express heartfelt thanks at worship gatherings as well as individually, from time to time, in response to commitments and gifts that are received.

Giving and gathering in the church is similar to all giving and getting in the kingdom. But it is clearly different as well. The intimacy of church life along with the church's central part in building Christ's kingdom makes it so. Done well, giving and getting in the church expands the kingdom, while nurturing the citizens of the kingdom. The result? Men and women who are better fit for the kingdom, here on earth, and yet to come.

> SHOWING GRATITUDE IS NOT ONLY THE RIGHT THING TO DO, IT IS THE NATURAL RESPONSE TO GOD'S WORK WITHIN A CHURCH FAMILY.

CHAPTER

HARD TOPICS FOR THE
CHRISTIAN FUNDRAISER

It just wouldn't be a picnic without the ants.
—Unknown

It should be no surprise that in the matter of giving and getting of resources there are paradoxes, tensions, and lots of room for discernment and critical judgment. Facing the issues and thinking through a principled stance on hard topics helps to ensure the integrity required of service in the kingdom.

ENDOWMENTS
Any seasoned fundraiser will tell you that there are some in the Christian tradition who resist the use of endowments to help fund ministry. There are people who cite ominous examples of the ruinous effect of endowments on theological integrity or the historic mission of Christian organizations.

A prime example is the older city church, long bereft of its role as salt and light in the community, barely hanging on to fifty members in a huge building that once served a parish of fifteen hundred people. How does it continue to exist though it is now largely irrelevant and impotent? The answer is it has accumulated funds in an endowment that enable it to survive—and even thrive financially—well past its vibrant service to Christ.

Another common example is Harvard University. The founding purpose of the oldest university in the United States, established in 1636, was the training of ministers of the gospel. The university long ago jettisoned its moorings to the Christian church (as have an unfortunate number of colleges and universities that were founded to serve the church), and some would claim that its endowment (now valued in the tens of billions) enables it to be untethered and unaccountable to its original constituency. That constituency would have been able, through its ongoing financial support (which it could choose to withhold), to enforce the university's fidelity to its Christian roots.

Despite such pitfalls, however, many Christian nonprofits have, or aspire to have, an endowment. What is an endowment?

An endowment is a fund, or series of funds, set aside and invested so that the earnings, or at least a portion of the earnings, can be a steady source of funding for the operation of the organization. For example, a mission organization might receive a $100,000 designated gift or provision of an estate to provide training for new missionaries. The mission could choose to spend $10,000 to 15,000 per year from that fund for the next seven years or so, expending the entire gift over a relatively short period of time.

Another mission might receive the same $100,000 designated for the same purpose. However, in consultation with the donor, they choose to use the gift differently. They invest the $100,000 with the goal of an average annual return of 8 percent. They further determine that each year they will use 5 percent of the earnings ($5,000 in the first year) toward the training of new missionaries. The other 3 percent ($3,000) will be placed back into the fund. The use of this $100,000 in an endowment can be summarized as follows:

$100,000 Endowment

Endowment and Spending Growth
Annual Endowment Return = 8%
Annual Endowment Spending Percentage = 5% of Prior Year's Ending Balance
Beginning Balance $100,000

Year	End of Year Balance (prior year's balance plus 8% less annual spending amount)	Annual Spending Amount (5% times prior year's balance)	Total Distributions
1	103,000	$5,000	5,000
2	106,090	5,150	10,150
3	109,273	5,305	15,455
4	112,551	5,464	20,918
5	115,927	5,628	26,546
6	119,405	5,796	32,342
7	122,987	5,970	38,312
8	126,677	6,149	44,462
9	130,477	6,334	50,796
10	134,392	6,524	57,319
11	138,423	6,720	64,039
12	142,576	6,921	70,960
13	146,853	7,129	78,089
14	151,259	7,343	85,432
15	155,797	7,563	92,995
16	160,471	7,790	100,784
17	165,285	8,024	108,808
18	170,243	8,264	117,072
19	175,351	8,512	125,584
20	180,611	8,768	134,352
30	242,726	11,783	237,877
40	326,204	15,835	377,006
50	438,391	21,281	563,984

Sample $100,000 endowment.

Which mission is the better steward? The first agency used the entire $100,000 gift in a relatively short period of time. The second agency, which received the same gift, used it for the same purpose but provided a steady and growing source of funds to help provide training in perpetuity. Note that in sixteen years (disregarding the time value of money in this illustration) the $100,000 endowment will have been paid out for the intended purpose. But note, too, that the endowment, after sixteen years, has an accrued value of $160,471 that is still at work for the intended purpose of the original gift. In year twenty, using our assumptions, there would be $180,611 in the endowment and the total amount paid out would be $134,352. In thirty years, $237,877 will have been paid out and $563,984 in fifty years, with $438,000 still available for future ministry!

I would argue that *both* organizations were good stewards, if their use of the gift aligned with the donor's purpose and organizational guidelines.

A POLICY OF NO ENDOWMENTS

Missionary Hudson Taylor famously said, "God's work, done in God's way, will never lack God's supply." Never a clearer statement in support of current giving for current ministry was ever spoken. While I would point out this is a human, not divine, declaration, it hews closely to the view that sustenance of ministry is tied to the will of its current constituency. Taylor's approach is appealing and defensible but hardly a mandate for a Christian organization intent on fidelity to Scripture and the tradition of the church.

Faith-based ministries that proudly declare they are not dependent upon endowments are not immune to straying from founding principles. The same type of "faith mission" can build physical or organizational structures in economically prosperous periods, or in response to unusually large occasional gifts, whose necessary upkeep in difficult economic periods can be debilitating to ministry and service opportunities.

A POLICY ENCOURAGING ENDOWMENTS

What practical considerations would favor establishing an endowment or series of endowments? First, donor intent should be considered. Some thoughtful stewards might determine they want their gift to be expended immediately, say, to provide the construction of a building to support the ministry. Another thoughtful steward might prefer to provide operational funds for the building in perpetuity through the establishment of an operating endowment. This would free the organization to apply future gifts to current needs and projects, rather than being saddled with the cost of maintaining the facility.

Second, the nature of the nonprofit enterprise should help determine whether, and in what amounts, to allow endowments. For example, an organization that provides microfinance opportunities for the very poor might be organized and equipped to offer loans from whatever amount is given in any particular year, which is likely to vary (say $250,000 in year one, $100,000 in year two, and $300,000 in year three). The small business loans can be easily scaled, either by the number or amount of loans given in any particular year.

Other more capital-intensive nonprofits, such as universities or hospitals, have large fixed costs that would be highly vulnerable to irregularities in the economic environment or annual gift totals if dependent upon steady and significant levels of gift income—with potentially disastrous consequences for those they seek to serve. For them, an endowment that would help smooth out necessary funding for ongoing operations might be integral to long-term fiscal health and effective pursuit of its mission.

In any case, the board of every nonprofit organization is responsible for setting guidelines for the financial health and integrity of their operations. Are there guidelines for use of endowments? Perhaps even

> THE BOARD OF EVERY NONPROFIT ORGANIZATION IS RESPONSIBLE FOR SETTING GUIDELINES FOR THE FINANCIAL HEALTH AND INTEGRITY OF THEIR OPERATIONS.

limits on what percentage of the operation can be funded by endowments, ensuring that there will always be reasonable dependence upon and accountability to the current constituency? One organization I know has written into their bylaws that the board must annually affirm the organization's theological orthodoxy—in this case, adherence to its public statement of faith. If the board cannot affirm the statement of faith, the bylaws state that the organization is required to transfer their endowment funds to another organization that *does* meet the established test of theological orthodoxy. That is a policy that can guard against the misuse of endowment funds.

Endowments are neither inherently evil nor inherently necessary. The wrong endowment of the wrong size for the wrong purpose can be spiritually dangerous, but the right one can be good stewardship. A policy of no endowments can allow current giving to guide the mission. Kingdom work can flourish with either policy. Like other matters of operations and governance, this issue must be carefully considered, guarded by good policy (how much, for what purposes, at what rate of payout, etc.), periodically evaluated, and clearly communicated to the supporting constituency.

RECOGNITION

It was a Sunday morning worship service, and the pastor had a special announcement to make to the congregation. There was an air of excitement in the room. The pastor joyfully pointed to the brand-new organ at the front of the auditorium. "Folks," he said, "we are the recipients of a marvelous gift. This beautiful organ, which will serve us well for generations to come, is the loving, generous gift of someone in our congregation. The donor was clear that this gift was to be strictly anonymous. It is God who should get the glory for this provision, not any person."

A clearly audible whisper came from the direction of one of the pews toward the back, "That's just the way I wanted it said."

While I doubt this story is factual, the conflicting sentiments ring true. In the realm of the kingdom, sharing recognition with the Giver of all good gifts is, if not anathema, then at least cause for some discomfort and self-reflection. Where does this sense of unease about recognition come from? Some would point to the Sermon on the Mount. Jesus said, "So when you give to the needy, do not announce it with trumpets, as the hypocrites do in the synagogues and on the streets, to be honored by men. I tell you the truth, they have received their reward in full" (Matthew 6:2). In light of this, is *any* recognition of a gift given in service to the kingdom appropriate?

> ENDOWMENTS ARE NEITHER INHERENTLY EVIL NOR INHERENTLY NECESSARY.

As is often the case, a closer examination makes the matter less simple. It is clear that Jesus is indicting *motives,* not necessarily the actions. The passage could not be clearer: if we give *in order to* receive the praise of men, we have indeed received our reward.

But in the same Sermon on the Mount, Jesus said, "Let your light shine before men, that they may see your good deeds and praise your Father in heaven" (Matthew 5:16–17). Is it possible that giving honor to a person for their faithful stewardship can bring glory to God and spur others to love and good works?

In a gathering of doctors who were contemplating their part in a new science facility at their alma mater, one of them, a doctor in his forties, shared a story. He said, "When I was a student, studying biology in our old science classroom, I looked up one day and saw a small plaque on the wall. It said something like, 'This classroom is provided by _____ to the glory of God and His service in this place.'" By now he had everyone's attention. "I said to myself that day," he continued, "that if God ever allows me to be a doctor, I will make a gift in gratitude for the education I am receiving here."

What can we infer from this example? First, the wording of the plaque makes it clear that the animating motive of the donor was to advance God's kingdom work at that place, not to congratulate himself on his generous gift. Second, that gift, given generations before the young premed student knew of it, was instrumental in someone else's thinking about his own stewardship.

One solution to the danger of human recognition stealing recognition from the Giver of all good gifts would be to offer no opportunity for recognition. However, this may be shortsighted and not as clearly in conformity with the teachings of Christ as it might appear on the surface. Indeed, it might be throwing out the baby of appropriate recognition with the bathwater of self-serving recognition.

Is there a middle way that acknowledges God's ultimate provision while giving thanks for the human agent(s) of that provision? If so, it requires great care by the getter and the giver alike. For the getter, the greatest danger is to appeal, whether subtly or overtly, to the unworthy motive of human recognition: "If you give $____, we will do ____." This kind of appeal does not hold up well to a biblical standard of conduct or to the highest and best reason to give. However, it does hold up to the biblical standard to say to a giver who has invested carefully in the kingdom work of your organization, "We know this is not why you gave the gift, but would you allow us to carefully recognize what God has led you to do? First, it will allow us as an organization to say thank you to you. That would be meaningful to *us*. Perhaps more important, the example of your giving could spur others to similar love and good works, not necessarily for our organization but for the sake of the kingdom!" It is also appropriate to honor a family member or mentor who made a spiritual mark on the donor's life. These are ways of laying "stones of remembrance" that can point others to what is good and right and worthy of praise.

For the giver, it may be a matter of spiritual maturity. Recognition, as a primary or maybe even important motivation for giving, is elevating the shallow and transitory rewards of this life above the eternal "well done" from God Himself. That sort of thinking betrays the lack of a kingdom perspective in the act of giving. There may be others whose unusual spiritual depth and understanding make the subject of any personal recognition uncomfortable at best. If someone is sincerely uncomfortable with being publicly recognized for their gift, the receiving organization, after gently asking permission to publicly say thank you, should graciously accept the wishes of the giver.

So is recognition ever appropriate? The easy answer is no. The more nuanced answer calls for discernment by the giver and getter alike. Leading a gift conversation with a naming opportunity is as offensive to the thoughtful Christian steward as it is to God Himself. Saying thank you appropriately, within the context of God's ultimate provision and glory, is not. The wise organization will think this matter through and establish guidelines that will inform the getter and the giver and protect the reputation of the Giver of all good gifts.

RECIPROCITY AND MIXED MOTIVES

Reciprocity, though we do not think about it often, is a powerful force in human interaction. Richard Thurnwald said, "The principle of reciprocity is the basis on which the entire social and ethical life of civilization rests." "Social equilibrium and cohesion," said Georg Simmel, "could not exist without the reciprocity of service and return service. All contacts among men rest on the scheme of giving and returning the equivalence."[15] Even Jesus said in the Sermon on the Mount, "Give, and it will be given to you" (Luke 6:38).

It took longer into my career than I care to admit to really think about the concept of reciprocity and the reality of mixed motives in the exercise of giving and getting. It might be a little like oxygen—mixed motives and reciprocity are so pervasive and ubiquitous in our daily social interactions that we rarely take note of their presence. But in the matter of giving and getting, concerns about motives and reciprocity appear frequently.

Why is the phrase "give back" such a pervasive part of our vocabulary? Why is there such a strong impulse to respond to a gift with a gift? Why, when we send a Christmas card to someone in late December, do we often get a card back from them within days? When someone honors us with their presence at a family wedding or funeral, why do we feel the (joyful) obligation to attend the next such event in their life? For that matter, where does the phrase "much obliged" come from? Why am I more inclined to offer to do the dishes when my wife rubs my back? Why is our first impulse upon receiving a gift to our organization to give something back—a thank-you, a small gift, the offer to name something?

It turns out that these strong impulses are an important element in the social fabric: families, friendships, business relationships, and even geopolitical relationships between nations all demonstrate aspects of the power and prevalence of reciprocity. Sociologists, anthropologists, psychologists, and even economists have explored the influence of reciprocity upon their disciplines.

For the purposes of this book, a detailed examination of this phenomenon is not required. But the principle of reciprocity and the motives underlying acts of reciprocity infuse the day-to-day work of giving and getting. The words *gratitude*, *pleasure*, *altruism*, *obligation*, and *self-interest* all orbit the topic of giving and getting. Consequently, motives and reciprocity deserve the attention and discernment of the thoughtful Christian steward.

In chapter 1 we observed the source of the need to give, namely, human response to God's gracious, unmerited gift and the intrinsic joy that emanates from giving. That gift can be observed every day in the natural creation all around us. Upon reflection, all of life and every breath is a gift of God. More particularly, in the kingdom, it is God's gift of grace in Christ Jesus on behalf of "those who are being saved" (2 Corinthians 2:15) that prompts the desire to give back.

Serge-Christophe Kolm is a leading scholar on the principle of reciprocity, particularly as it bears upon economics. He identifies three levels of reciprocity: *Propriety*—those things we do for social balance and fairness (think Christmas cards); *Liking*—those things we do because we like a particular person or organization and (lurking somewhere in there) wanting to be liked for our liking (think of buying magazine subscriptions in support of your neighbor girl's soccer league—because you support community sports teams and you want to be thought well of by your neighbors, even though you didn't know *Popular Mechanics* was still being published!); and *Self-interest*—giving in return to elicit another gift (think of sending flowers to a key donor on her birthday, both because there is genuine love and affection for this person and because you hope that a warm relationship will eventuate into a future gift). It is easy to see how reciprocity and mixed motives reside in, under, and through many human interactions.[16]

Simply being aware of the principle of reciprocity can help the giver and the getter alike to be generous as well as pure in heart in the giving and receiving of gifts. How can the principle of reciprocity taint a magnificent gift? Let's presume the need for a gift of a brand-new building for the central offices of your organization. All would agree that the highest and best reason for this gift would be to enable the kingdom-centered mission of the organization to move forward

> SIMPLY BEING AWARE OF THE PRINCIPLE OF RECIPROCITY CAN HELP THE GIVER AND THE GETTER ALIKE TO BE GENEROUS AS WELL AS PURE IN HEART IN THE GIVING AND RECEIVING OF GIFTS.

with greater efficiency and vigor. But might there be lesser, even harmful motives lurking behind this gift? For the giver, is there a need to be recognized or thanked? Is the gift timed to show displeasure with previous administrations of the organization? Was there a particular tax advantage to the gift that could as easily have precluded the gift?

Did the recipient organization present this gift opportunity to the eventual donor out of true institutional need or in competition with another nonprofit? Were kingdom values preeminent in the discussions with the donor or were appeals made to lesser motives like recognition or salving conscience for a financial windfall? Did the organization's representative presume to know God's will about the giver's obligation to the project or humbly present the opportunity with care and respect for the donor's own conscience before God?

The purpose of this discussion is not to resolve all ambiguity about motives in the giving and getting of gifts. Life is too complicated for that. But the wise giver and getter will understand that in this fallen world, complex motives coupled with the powerful force of reciprocation require discernment and awareness. Can a gift be manipulative? Can a request for a gift appeal to lesser motives rather than greater? Of course. Strain toward the best and purest in giving and getting. This is part of what it means to guard our hearts (chapter 6). If we make ourselves aware of the ambiguities of motives and the pitfalls of reciprocity, we are better equipped to give and to get in a matter worthy of the kingdom.

ORGANIZATIONAL MISSION AND DONOR PASSION

A recurring tension in giving and getting is balancing, and sometimes adjudicating, organizational vision with the stewardship passions of the individual. This side of eternity, there can be dissonance in matching what is best for the organization with the animating passions of the thoughtful Christian steward.

A Christian grammar school is providing excellent education for its K–6 students, as it has for many years. A donor approaches the headmaster. "I'd like to give a substantial gift to enable you to move toward being a K–12 school. I can't give you the whole amount necessary, but I can give you more than half of what you would need."

This is a point of decision for the school. On the one hand, a multimillion dollar gift would be, by far, the biggest gift in their history. It would probably increase attendance at the grammar school while propelling the whole enterprise to greater prominence in the community. Besides, this giver has been a longtime supporter of the school. On the other hand, what is the mission of the grammar school? Is there need in the community for more private Christian education at the 7–12 grade level? Does the present board and administration have the expertise to pull this off?

Every organization will face opportunities like this, some larger, some seemingly much smaller. But which ones are God-given opportunities and which ones would only serve to broaden (or even change) your mission and thus dilute your effectiveness to the kingdom? Sometimes the most courageous decision an organization can make is to turn down a gift. As hard as it might be to say no to a gift, it may be the very best thing for the future of the organization. It comes back to mission and purpose. If an organization is well-grounded in its mission, it is easier to say yes to new ideas that advance that mission and easier to say no to ideas that will divert you from the very reason you exist.

While saying no to a gift is never easy, it provides an opportunity for the organization to reaffirm its mission. Saying no is also a way an organization can help a thoughtful giver direct his or her stewardship in a more meaningful direction. Saying no to a gift is not denying money to the kingdom, if you are able to direct the giver to a kingdom ministry that better fits their own vision for faithful stewardship. Any Christian enterprise that is contributing to the kingdom has an obligation to be true to its mission, even if it means redirecting a potential gift to another organization that can better fulfill the passion of the giver. It may be counterintuitive, but it is in keeping with service in the kingdom.

CONSULTANTS

Gathering for the kingdom cannot be haphazard or relegated to wishful thinking. It takes large measures of thought, prayer, planning, and sheer effort to effectively call even the most gifted givers to advance the mission of our organization. In the rhythm of organizational life, there are times when it is prudent and necessary to seek outside counsel. What are some of the cues that indicate when to seek outside counsel? Who do we hire? How do we best manage a relationship with outside counsel?

> SOMETIMES THE MOST COURAGEOUS DECISION AN ORGANIZATION CAN MAKE IS TO TURN DOWN A GIFT.

When is it time to bring in outside counsel?

Seeking outside counsel is not an admission of weakness. In fact, it is a way strong organizations can test their thinking and shape their planning for the greatest benefit of the organization. What are the points at which counsel might be appropriate?

It might be at the point of organizing your development effort. A consultant has observed scores of organizational structures from the inside. Consultants have seen poor allocation of human resources and operational budgets and they have seen effective allocation. You can also test your assessment of your people and programs by retaining competent and experienced outside counsel.

New initiatives or campaigns are another time when an objective viewpoint can facilitate good planning (chapter 12). Objective conversations with key stakeholders (feasibility study), advice to the CEO and board on timing, organization, and size of the goal can be an invaluable tool. It can also accelerate the planning process and get you underway in a timely manner.

How do you find good counsel?

There are so many firms and individual consultants that it is difficult to pore through directories, for example, in *The Chronicle of Philanthropy*. A good way to get started is to talk to other similar nonprofits that you admire. Have they been through a campaign like the one you anticipate? Have they ever brought in counsel to conduct an audit of their development program? Talking to others and learning of their experience with specific counsel can be your most reliable guide to a consultant that will fit with you and your organization. But conduct face-to-face interviews with at least three firms (or individuals) before you decide. And depending on the project you have in mind, it is always wise to have a group of people from your organization attend the presentation from each firm. You will get a better feel for fit from a broader range of people who know your institution well. Find out the services they are contracting to provide and the outcomes they intend to deliver. Evaluate and compare costs, as they can differ greatly. Most important, make sure you are talking to the very person (or people) who will be delivering the service. Sometimes larger firms will send their president or top salesman for the presentation but provide someone previously unknown to you as counsel. Getting the best counsel usually involves great care in the selection process.

What does a healthy engagement of counsel look like?

What should you expect from a relationship with counsel? First and foremost, you should expect experience and expertise. You should also make sure they will tell you the truth—always. I've always told counsel I have hired that their honest opinion is what we are paying them for, and they are free to make even negative assessments to the president or board members, as long as they disclose those assessments to the head of the department they are evaluating. But close to experience and truth-telling in importance is *partnership*. We engage counsel to improve the performance of our organization in winning friends and financial support. Clinical data and assessment is helpful, but if you find a sincere partner whose goal is to help you succeed, you have found a valuable resource that is worth the cost and time of the engagement.

OUR PART, GOD'S PART

A relative from a big city was visiting his uncle's farm. As he looked with wonder on the lush, cultivated field of grain, the meticulous rows totally cleared of weeds, the visitor exclaimed, "You and God have sure created a beautiful thing."

The farmer dryly replied, with a glimmer in his eye, "Yea, you should have seen it when God had it all to Himself!"

The work of getting in the kingdom is a collaboration. It is a collaboration between the gatherer and the giver. It is a collaboration between the mission of the organization and the mission of the donor. But at a more fundamental level, gathering on behalf of the kingdom is the work of God in and through organizations and people in building His kingdom and its inhabitants.

God doesn't *need* us to accomplish His work in this world, but He has chosen to use us for that purpose. It is a high privilege to call God's people to invest their treasure in people and programs that have eternal value in God's sight. To return to a recurring theme in the matter of giving and getting in the kingdom, we must always remember that our part is important. We must plant and water. But make no mistake, "it is God who gives the increase."

AFTERWORD

SHREWD AS **SNAKES, INNOCENT** AS DOVES

When Jesus talked with His disciples about how to make their way in this world without His physical presence, His instruction was pithy and profound: "Be shrewd as snakes and innocent as doves" (Matthew 10:16). In fact, Jesus forewarned His disciples that, in this world, they would be as "sheep among wolves" in their service to the kingdom.

Surely Jesus knew that these and future disciples of His would face indifference or even active opposition to His claim of lordship over all. The human heart, desperately self-centered, does not naturally welcome the message that God's Word is true and Christ's kingdom will ultimately prevail. To make one's way, at least on this side of His eternal kingdom, the disciple will face elements of a hostile environment that require a savvy understanding of the human heart and the ways of the world, coupled with the childlike innocence of a person wholly given over to the Lord Jesus Christ. In this world we are called to be both shrewd and innocent in the matter of giving and getting in the kingdom.

WHO IS THE TRUE GIVER?

The true giver is not captive to whim or emotion. They have a godly shrewdness. They listen with the heart *and* the brain. They are not moved to give solely because of a winsome presentation or a promised outcome. Their will to give is coupled with probing, honest questions. Is the plan credible? Can the organization pull it off?

True givers ensure that their giving is in alignment with their God-given passions and goals. They carefully evaluate whether God has put them in a financial position and prepared their heart to help fund the proposed endeavor.

The true giver asks good questions. Careful stewards model their master by probing to discover the true meaning and intent of the asker. They seek to discern if the representative of the organization is authentic and sincere and if there is a credible need and opportunity. They look for a history of effective stewardship. And they probe for measurable goals, contingency plans, and a track record of achievement that warrants investment.

But the true giver does not exhibit shrewdness alone. They have an innocent quality as well. True givers ask for and allow God's Spirit to direct giving decisions, even in areas that are new to their thinking and experience. They test their own motives. Is recognition or influence driving the decision to give, or is the call of God upon their resources? The true giver cares about, but is not consumed with, demonstrable results. Rather, they have a childlike willingness to "cast their bread upon the waters" in obedience to Christ. They lean more heavily toward giving without calculation than figuring safe, attainable giving commitments. And if the decision is no, they are careful to deny the request in a manner that encourages and instructs the ministry and the messenger.

> TRUE GIVERS ASK FOR AND ALLOW GOD'S SPIRIT TO DIRECT GIVING DECISIONS, EVEN IN AREAS THAT ARE NEW TO THEIR THINKING AND EXPERIENCE.

WHO IS THE TRUE FUNDRAISER?

Shrewdness is characteristic of the true fundraiser too. The wise getter carefully gathers as much information as possible about the potential steward. What is their animating passion? What is their capacity to give? What are their other giving interests? The fundraiser carefully discerns how the cause they represent aligns with the priorities of the donor. If it does not, the true gatherer encourages the steward to be rich toward God in a way that is in accord with *their* God-given passions, even if it means directing their gift to another organization. The wise getter determines a project and dollar goal that makes sense for the potential donor. She listens, she adjusts, and she calls for commitment. She is as anxious to learn as to educate and ask. She values a lifetime relationship of the ministry to the donor above the immediacy of any goal or particular project.

> IT IS TIME FOR THE TRUE FUNDRAISER TO CONFIDENTLY CALL THOUGHTFUL STEWARDS TO USE THEIR GIFTS IN HIS SERVICE.

The true fundraiser never forgets to report the results of the gift to the donor—one week later, one year later, five years later, and longer. And she never, ever, fails to say, "Thank you."

But there is an innocence about the Christian fundraiser as well. He approaches every contact with a potential giver in utter dependence upon Christ to superintend the conversation and the outcome. In deference to the thoughtful steward, he thoroughly prepares for every interaction. He is always more willing to listen than to persuade. While bold to ask, he is graciously willing to receive a no and continue to value the relationship. Service to the donor is far more important than a gift to the organization. The true fundraiser never measures the care and friendship extended to the donor by the degree of financial response to the solicitation. Every relationship is an opportunity for ministry. And *every* gift is an occasion for thanksgiving to God.

The universal calling of followers of Christ is to be rich toward God in all we possess—time, talent, and treasure. The eternal values of Christ's kingdom require the true giver to be bold. Likewise, the ministry of calling God's people to be rich toward God is a sacred trust that extends beyond a particular ministry, a particular time, and a particular need into the realm of the fullness of Christ's kingdom itself. It is time for the true fundraiser to confidently call thoughtful stewards to use their gifts in His service. Anything less, whether giving or getting, is unworthy of the kingdom.

The giver and the getter must happily and thoughtfully embrace the joy of giving and the joy of getting—not as an obligation but as the privilege of participation in Christ's kingdom. To give ourselves wholeheartedly in this way to Christ's kingdom is a noble and worthy calling. So let's get on with it!

NOTES

1. Randy Alcorn, *The Treasure Principle: Unlocking the Secret of Joyful Giving* (Colorado Springs: Multnomah, 2001), 50.
2. John Beardsley, "A Model of Christian Charity," Winthrop Society, accessed April 2011, http://religiousfreedom.lib.virginia.edu/sacred/charity.html.
3. Cotton Mather, *Essays to Do Good* (London: William and Sons, Stationers' Court; and Burton and Briggs, 1816), 27.
4. William Penn, *No Cross, No Crown* (London: Mary Hinde, 1771), 241.
5. Alexis de Tocqueville, *Democracy in America* (1945; repr., New York: Alfred A. Knopf, 1973).
6. Os Guinness, *Doing Well and Doing Good: Money, Giving, and Caring in a Free Society* (Colorado Springs: NavPress, 2001), 139.
7. Robert L. Payton, *Philanthropy: Voluntary Action for the Public Good* (New York: Macmillan, 1988), 135.
8. Ibid., 45.
9. Ibid., 105.
10. Ibid.,136.
11. A. T. Pierson, "Two Amazing Accounts of George Mueller, and Prayer," Puritan Fellowship, accessed April 2011, last modified February 7, 2008, http://www.puritanfellowship.com/ 2008/02/two-amazing-accounts-of-george-mueller.html.

12. Michael S. Hamilton, "More Money, More Ministry: The Financing of American Evangelicalism Since 1945," in *More Money, More Ministry: Money and Evangelicals in Recent North American History*, ed. Larry Eskridge and Mark A. Noll (Grand Rapids: Eerdmans, 2000), 106.

13. Thomas J. Stanley and William D. Danko, *The Millionaire Next Door: The Surprising Secrets of America's Wealthy* (New York: Simon & Schuster, 1996).

14. Os Guinness, *The Call: Finding and Fulfilling the Central Purpose of Your Life* (Nashville: Thomas Nelson, 1998), 4.

15. Serge-Christophe Kolm, *Reciprocity: An Economics of Social Relations* (New York: Cambridge University Press, 2008), v.

16. Ibid., chapter 5.

ACKNOWLEDGMENTS

I am profoundly grateful to President Philip Ryken and the Board of Trustees of Wheaton College for providing a sabbatical in early 2011. It is not that common for administrators to be afforded this kind of respite, but it provided the time I needed to reflect and write. I doubt this volume would have come to be without this generous gift.

My wife, Susan, poured over many early drafts, and offered invaluable (and gentle) insight. Thank you, sweetheart.

Anna Walsh, my very capable assistant, was always patiently and cheerfully available to secure resource materials, edit content, and format endless drafts. Her joy at the completion of this project will be almost as great as mine.

In thirty years of gathering funds for kingdom purposes, I have met hundreds of people who have taught me what it means to give in a manner worthy of the Lord Jesus Christ. I have also worked side by side with many who have showed me how to gather resources in a winsome and God-honoring way. I am a better person, professional, husband, and father for their example, counsel, and friendship. I am blessed and forever grateful for each one.

As I gathered my thoughts and put them to paper, I asked a very special group of men and women to guide me by reviewing and responding to my work. I offer my thanks to Julie Bullock, Adam Carr,

Louise Furrow, Jim Krall, Kurt Keilhacker, Don Meyer, Phil Ryken, Tom Schmidt, Michael Sinkus, Joe Stowell, and Mark and Kathy Vaselkiv. I have learned much from their feedback, and their example.

I am indebted to Michael Hamilton for first introducing me to the juxtaposition of George Mueller and D. L. Moody as archetypes of two approaches to funding for Christian ministry.

May this small offering guide many to more joyful and fruitful service in the eternal kingdom of the Lord Jesus Christ.